An Unconventionally C

THE GREATNESS IN YOU

How unleashing your infinite potential unlocks infinite possibilities for you

Seanaphoka Tsapi

First published in South Africa by Reach Publishers, 2015

ISBN 978 086 9707753
eISBN 978-0-620-66144-7

Book Editor
Pamela Kauffman

Book Cover Branding and Design:
Studio 40

BOOK AVAILABLE IN:

Paperback Edition

Corporate Gift Edition

Amazon Kindle Edition

Audio CD

E-Book

CONTENTS

PREFACE

In each and every one of us is a talent, a gift, a purpose and a sole reason for why we are here. The ability to not only awaken to this reality and to allow ourselves to unleash our talents to the world means discovering our inner greatness. This book seeks to ignite that spark in you to create an inferno of greatness that will one day illuminate the world. It is my believe that each of us is destined for greatness in life. This conviction has served as a springboard for my writing of this book and I am grateful to those people who, through their inspiring work and lives, have helped me put this book together.

Soon you will find the key to your purpose, your greatness. It may or not be in the number of degrees you will achieve. When you find it, don't whisper it into my ear, go out there into the world and share with the world, because it could be. To live a meaningful life, share your talents with the world. For in this world, the only way to reach the heights of greatness is to strive for the depths of service to the people around you. In the land of the blind, the one eyed shall be king; however, in this world we live in, the enlightened is the messenger, so seek to be a servant and not a king, for servants live a nobler life. Life is too precious a gift to live it in a moment as short as a lifetime, live it forever.

A fruit borne as a result of the seeds of inspiration planted in me, the inspiration to write this book has been drawn from many great people whom I have known through their work and lived to learn about in my curiosity and my quest to learn about success, a concept gnawing at my mind since I first heard the word. Having a purpose seems to have puzzled many people in the world and yet it is fulfilled by only a handful. Great people, during their brief visits here on Earth, although they seemed to have lived decades, centuries and millennia apart, have had one belief in common, one philosophy. They seemed to have upheld one message, or perhaps one principle. This one thread of belief seems to have connected these great spirits across time and in their own words they will help you to unleash *The Greatness in You.*

The promise of this book is to provide you with the outlook, principles and stories of people who have applied these principles in life, therefore achieving their dreams and unleashing their potential in life. This book intends to help you overcome all the inhibitors that have impeded you from realising how talented you are, how gifted and great you were born to be.

This book's promise to you is that you will be inspired to become a better person, to achieve more and be more in this world, to reach your greatest potential. It will encourage you to charge boldly to your dreams and turn them into reality and, most importantly, empower you to become the best that you are destined to be. As you learn the principles enshrined in this book and apply them daily in your life, you will be taking bold steps to transform your life into the success that you have always wanted to be. The greatness in you is waiting for you to unleash it, to tap into your infinite power, to unlock all those possibilities and opportunities that will enable you to live the life to which you have always aspired.

All that you have dreamed of, all that you have ever wanted to have and become in your life resides nowhere but within you. The power to then bring those dreams into reality is in you. You are the fire that burns the torch to your dreams; you are the future that you envision, the greatness that you aspire for. The resources and means to acquire all that you have always dreamed of for your life are in you. The question then that remains is how do you tap into this power in you to open this new world for you to live in?

The Greatness in You – How unleashing your infinite potential, unlocks infinite possibilities for you takes you through a journey of self-discovery. As you weave the principles in this book into the fabric of your life, you give yourself the opportunity to discover, explore and achieve your potential. This book aims to help you unleash the power within you to realise your own dreams by helping you cultivate a great sense of belief in yourself and understand why this belief is so important. You will discover that the word 'limit' is relative to what you believe about your potential and what you can achieve. The book also emphasises the importance of the power of a positive mental attitude to lead you to achieving greatness in life.

When the time is right, you will come right. And perhaps you realise that the countdown has begun. It is my hope that this book will fulfill its promise to you, that it will remind you of the abundance, health, joy and wealth already in the palms of your hands as you overcome all the factors that hinder you from claiming what is rightfully yours. By the time you finish this book, you will have learned how to apply the principles in this book to yield positive and desirable outcomes in your life. The sole purpose of this book is to help you tap into your resourcefulness, overcome your fears, embrace your innate gifts, take control of your life, and your destiny. Be the great person you were born to be. Never believe anyone who says your dreams and goals are impossible, because they are in fact possible. Therefore the difference between where you are right now and where you aspire to be is in your ability to

DARE TO DREAM, DARE TO DO IT!

ACKNOWLEDGMENTS

This book owes much of its message to the people who inspired its writing. If I ever see afar in life, it is because of these giants who lend me their shoulders to stand on.

In memoriam of my beloved grandmother, in the words of Rick Bragg, "*This is a place where grandmothers hold babies on their laps under the stars and whisper in their ears that the stars are holes in the floor of the sky.*"

To my mother, as a Jewish proverb appraises, "*God could not be everywhere, and therefore he made mothers.*"

To my nearest and dearest friend, Palesa; otherwise formally known as my CEO (Chief Emotional Officer), thank you for your invaluable input and suggestions into this book.

As we grow older, our friends become our family and our family become our friends. Mzukisi Dyasi, Rethabile Seshabela, Raymond Hape Sedikane, Thuto Makuta, Disebo Ranoha, Dikhabiso Motsamai, Refiloe Tsenoli, Morapeli Rametsi, Lesi Rapetswa, Deshy Sebola, Tebogo Manaka, Orateng Maetle and Kgosi Mashego - all your dreams will come to fruition.

In the words of William Ward, "The mediocre teacher tells. The good teacher explains. The superior teacher demonstrates. The great teacher inspires." To Mr. Japie Moropa, Stefan Diedericks, Victor Gabuza, Sedrick Theodosiou, Adolph Kaestner and Cyril Tshabalala; I am truly grateful for your ongoing inspiration, support, teachings and advice. You have provided a moral compass and guiding light both in my professional and personal endeavours.

To the Editor of this work, Pamela Kauffman; thank you for preserving my voice in this book, and therefore my song. To the Reach Publishers team for making this project a reality. Thank you all for your tireless efforts in lending your talents, skills and experience in making it possible for this book to reach the hands of the reader.

In the end, this book was inspired by the works and lives of the people who through their achievements and deeds continue to inspire each of us to reach for greatness ourselves. These men and women who stood out in society and did outstanding things with their lives. The least we can do is to learn from them and use those valuable lessons as a lantern to illuminate the paths that lead us to our own destinies.

This book is dedicated to THE GREATNESS IN YOU.

Whatever the height of imagination and dreams your mind can reach, then the depth of your courage and capabilities can manifest.

A Special *Creed* from the Author to You

DISCOVERING THE GREATNESS IN YOU

Growing up is about experiences. They make you strong; teach you more and more as you continue to conquer the course of life. I have come to realise that nothing is too difficult to achieve in life, nor it is too easy. The first principle to personal success and potential discovery is to believe in yourself, believe in your goals and, most importantly, be prepared to fight, to persist... to persevere.

Life is nothing but a piece of art that has a sort of fascinating science behind it... It is good to be alive. However, the most important thing is being lively, setting your own trend and living it. Most people see challenges as problems instead of potholes that can be covered with a simple concrete foundation, which sets as a breakthrough point for the conqueror. You live life, then why do you think it can for a moment control and limit your human creative potential, integrity, intelligence and your capabilities to achieve what you want to be and beyond, to be successful.

Most people give up even before they try. It is as much effort to lose as it is to win. Self-esteem and self-discipline are the first principles to overcoming fear, which is the barrier to discovering your potential for success. Every day presents to you a new discovery, experience, challenge and, most importantly, opportunity.

Ambition leads to greater fulfillment on an individual basis as you use your imagination to create new horizons and frontiers for what you do in your life. As you imagine what you could be and achieve, you move beyond the boundaries you have previously set for yourself. Ambition therefore has a novelty and also relevance in terms of changing what you do and what you believe about your potential, which is yet to be realised. *They say, "The sky is the limit."* The actual truth is that the only limits you have in life are the ones you impose on yourself.

They say, "*Strike while the iron is still hot.*" This time, take my advice, *Strike it until it's hot.* The most beautiful thing about life is when you realise that you do not have limits that you can achieve whatever you want provided you channel all your energy, effort, time, intellect and passion in achieving it. When your dreams and ambitions become your purpose for living, you become absolutely unstoppable and persevering.

In conclusion to this credo I would like to say to you, '*There is no wealth more rewarding than education and information. Seek it, find it and it will enlighten and liberate you forever.*' Moreover, there is nothing wrong with dreaming or being a big dreamer. In fact, you should embrace it and nourish it. For *imagination is an endless journey of countless discoveries* and to those who will purport to realise the reality of their dreams may I say confidently to you, 'Bon voyage!'

INTRODUCTION

"Success is not an overnight journey; it's a lifetime goal…"

What is greatness? The definitions are varied and relative to each individual's perception of the world. Each definition is entirely dependent upon a person's perception of life. However, among all definitions, one hits closest to home. The most profound definition of success is this: success is a gradual and incremental achievement of a meaningful ideal. In the words of Patanjali this means, "*When you are inspired by some great purpose, some extraordinary project, all your thoughts break their bonds: your mind transcends limitations, your consciousness expands in every direction and you find yourself in a new, great and wonderful world. Dormant forces, faculties and talents become alive, and you discover yourself to be a greater person by far than you ever dreamed yourself to be.*" Success is therefore the innate courage to discover the power, potent dreams and potential that have lain within you from birth.

Many people say, "I want to be successful in the future; I want to be successful tomorrow." The truth is you can definitely be successful in the future solely because the most beautiful thing about the future is that it comes one day at a time. What you do today will pave the way for what you become tomorrow. Therefore every day brings you a step closer to being the person you ultimately want to be. Take today as an opportunity to become better than you were yesterday, and take today as an opportunity to become better tomorrow than you are today. More often people say, "I am going to take a break today, I will work harder tomorrow." But every day we take a break from pursuing our life goals, those goals are postponed as well by one more day.

Two colleagues, upon leaving the office at the end of the day, one asked her friend, "Linda, what does success mean to you? When are you going to say you are living your dream?" The friend replied, "William, my friend, good is not good enough any more. Dreams are not those things you have when you go to sleep. Dreams are those things you can no longer go to sleep because you've got to have them…" Linda elaborated, "As you think you are creating, as you say it with the voice of your heart, you are foretelling it and as you act upon it, you are definitely making it happen, making it come true. When it comes to achieving your dreams, forget about going the extra mile, go all the way. Even when obstacles hinder you from achieving your goals, keep on walking." What is even more amazing about going beyond the extra mile and doing more than is expected of you is the discovery of new opportunities, the opening up of new possibilities and exploring new frontiers. Those who say that there is light at the end of the tunnel, usually they are missing out on the light that is actually in the tunnel. Always bear in your mind and heart that the road to success is always under construction and the journey in itself is the reward.

THE MAGIC OF BELIEVING IN YOU

Self-belief, a positive attitude and, most importantly, a confident approach and view of everything around you is key for personal success. What you see is what matters, so see the positive. Some people see obstacles every day of their lives and other people see opportunities in those obstacles. How you see things around you, your self-belief, determines your success. The most important thing is having a conviction that you will succeed regardless of any circumstances. A Japanese sword master had a student, Miyomoto Musashi, who from the age of seven wanted to grow up to be the best sword-fighter in his province. His master told him, "*Look at everything that is negative from a positive perspective and learn to view everything that is positive from a beautiful perspective. Life is beautiful, not just in these two ways, but in many ways.*"

Miyomoto's teacher taught him that if he wanted something in life, if he really wanted to master the art of swordsmanship, if he wanted to be a warrior, if he wanted that honour and power, he had to ask himself daily what was he doing every day, every hour, that would serve as a step to getting him there. What efforts would he take every hour to bring him closer to his dreams? Because what he wanted was already there, waiting for him. With a relentless need in his spirit to reach the height of greatness, Miyomoto travelled to different provinces to learn from other swordsmen and strategists. His first real sword fight was when he was thirteen and he defeated the strategist of the Shinto school. This victory fuelled his belief he could become the greatest strategist and swordsman and he went on to defeat many other opponents.

After many years and many fights, Miyomoto realised his childhood dream of being an accomplished swordsman, known and respected across all the provinces of Japan. At the age of fifty, he wrote his book on strategy, *The Book of Five Rings*, which begins by reflecting back on his life and accomplishments.

"When I reached thirty, I looked back on my past. The previous victories were not due to my having mastered strategy. Perhaps it was natural ability, or that the other school's strategy was inferior. After that I studied morning and evening, searching for the principle, and I came to realise the 'Way of Strategy' when I was fifty.

"Since then I have lived without following any particular Way. Thus with the virtue of strategy I practise many arts and abilities, all things with no teacher. To write this book I did not use the law or the teachings of Confucius, neither did I use old war chronicles nor books on martial tactics. I took up my brush to explain the true spirit of this Ichi School as it is mirrored in the Way of Kwannon. This time is the night of the tenth day of the tenth month, at the hour of the tiger (which is 3-5 a.m. in modern language)."

What Miyomoto did consciously for many years of his life was believe in himself. He believed in his vision and most importantly he believed in his ability to bring that dream to reality. He never for a second doubted himself and his abilities. He knew that anything he virtually desired in this world could be his as long as he cultivated in himself the firmness of knowing that he was without doubt destined to achieve it. Miyomoto knew the power that lay in believing in himself. He knew that the road to his success began with belief in himself and the place he rightly belonged to in the world. He had no time for debates, arguments or explanations. He set out to become a great strategist and swordsman, and he stood behind that dream until he realised it.

"As a person appraises, in his soul, so he is."
Jewish Proverb

Five hundred years later *A Book of Five Rings* is still a fundamental book on strategy for academics and business leaders alike. His vision and the principles he used to achieve his dream have become a guidebook Fortune 500 executives use to turn their organisational visions into reality. Miyomoto started with nothing but the power to believe in himself and his dream. In his world, he became a superman primarily because he had supernormal beliefs about himself and his abilities.

"The inferno of the living is not something that will be; if there is one, it is what is already here, the inferno where we live every day, that we form by being together. There are two ways to escape suffering it. The first is easy for many: accept the inferno and become such a part of it that you can no longer see it. The second is risky and demands constant vigilance and apprehension: seek and learn to recognise who and what, in the midst of inferno, are not inferno, then make them endure, give them space."
Italo Calvino

Let's reflect on the life of a noble man who changed his country, his continent, and the world at large. A respected statesman and the first president of a democratic South Africa, Mr. Nelson Mandela, on the day he received his life sentence, made it very clear what he stood for and what he believed in. He firmly believed in his ideal to the point where he was willing to lose his life for it; he had set a definite goal in his life and he worked progressively towards it. More often people set goals in their lives and lack the ongoing commitment and discipline to see things through. How many people do you know who believe in their dreams to that degree? He believed that one day his country and his people would live in peace in a democratic and free society with equal opportunities, irrespective of their race or background.

Of course having that kind of belief in South Africa in that era was no different from Galileo's belief in the sixteenth century that the world was round and the sun was the centre of the universe. That kind of belief was thought of as poisonous and unhealthy to the country. Having stood for what he believed in, Nelson Mandela was tried in court, charged with treason and sentenced to life imprisonment, the result of standing too firmly on his beliefs. He held on to his belief amidst trials and tribulations; served twenty-seven years in prison, and was released in 1990. His dream became a reality not only in South Africa but also in the world at large. This belief, this level of certainty, fuelled his courage and made it easy for him to tolerate and stand against any challenges that tried to divert him from his vision. Ultimately his strength of belief led to his success.

THE POWER OF A POSITIVE ATTITUDE

A positive state of the mind is a set of optimistic views, values, strategies and habits or notions that are held by an individual in such a way that a compelling incentive is established in their mental framework to continue to adopt certain behaviours and decisions to achieve success in their lives. As it is, success in all of its forms is a matter of choice and not chance. A positive mindset is an appealing outlook about life and everything in it. The ability to create personal beliefs about the opportunity in everything and having an "*I can do better than that*" outlook or philosophy about life is positive thinking. Positive thinking goes hand in hand with success.

An inspiring story on positive attitude is one celebrated in the United States of America. Horatio Alger's Ragged Dick is an extraordinarily optimistic young gentleman who started life on the streets of New York when, at the tender age of three, his parents passed on and he had no one to care for him.

Like every other street child, he had to survive despite the odds. He took up the profession of a shoe shiner to complement his profession and, of course, his standard of living. Dick had quite a dismal appearance. The oversized clothing he wore and the dirty scuffmarks on his face earned him the name Ragged Dick.

Ragged Dick acquired skill as a bootblack and commenced each day with enthusiasm. Due to his honesty and friendliness, he attracted many customers and earned enough money to get by. On good days, Dick spent his extra earnings watching plays at the theatre in the evenings; at times he generously invited a friend to join him.

Dick's ragged days eventually came to an end; he wore a new suit on his back and was given $5, the highest amount of money he had ever earned and which he put to good use. His first objective was to rent a room to avoid sleeping in boxes on the street. He then opened a savings account and started saving money. This was a street child with a strong sense of responsibility and a hunger to succeed. He never again wore ragged clothing and was always clean and professional in appearance.

One working day Dick met another young fellow on the street. His name was Henry Fosdick. Henry was once well cared for and obtained an education before his parents passed away. Dick offered Henry accommodation and in return Henry helped Dick study in the evenings. He taught him how to read, write, a bit of geography and some arithmetic here and there. It was no challenge for Henry, Dick was a quick learner and very intelligent. The two boys lived together harmoniously and continued to educate and liberate each other to become better people.

Dick's days on the street as a boot-black soon came to an end when the young man's swimming skills earned him a well-deserved break. Mr. James Rockwell was more than honoured to reward Dick with a proper job as a clerk at his counting house after he selflessly jumped into the cold water to save Mr. Rockwell's son who had accidentally fallen off a moving ferry. Dick's heroic actions ensured that Mr. Rockwell had no objection to giving Dick the job. Later he learned that the young chap had obtained an education despite all odds. Dick's good fortune was well deserved after all.

In this incredible story, Horatio Alger teaches us that life may not pan out the way you planned it. However, you have the pan in your hands anyway so make the best out of it. In all good turns things will work out. Every situation is a golden opportunity as long as you cultivate a golden attitude. To honour this story, a Horatio Alger Award is given to a rags to riches individual in the United Stated Of America for exemplifying outstanding dedication, purpose, and perseverance in their personal lives.

"There is a little difference in people, but that little difference makes a big difference. That little difference is ATTITUDE. The big difference is whether it is positive or negative."

W. Clement Stone

All that you are today and all that you will ever be tomorrow are entirely dependent upon your state of the mind. Your thoughts hold within them the power to change your current reality. As you think, your thoughts are like energy, which communicates to the universe, and ultimately it conspires to your desires. Gravitate more to positive thoughts in your everyday life as this has a natural power to yield positive results in your life.

Your current reality is a tangible manifestation of your thoughts; therefore guard your thoughts carefully, as they are like a tree that bears the fruits of your life. Cultivate and nourish the habit of dwelling on good thoughts, soak your mind with thoughts of greatness, success, health and abundance in your life and your intuition will propel you to a reality which you desire from your innermost heart instead of your fears. You attract into your life both what you fear most and desire most.

The reality one must accept is that there is more you can give to this world than you can take from it; use your talents and gifts to make this world a better place. Ask not what the world can do for you; ask yourself what you can do for the world. When you invest your thoughts in this powerful question, you transcend from being a mediocre individual to one purpose driven, which energises your spirit and fuels your courage to do better and become better. Your thoughts are the clay with which you mould your world. Your belief in your thoughts and your faith in them are the driving force, the fire, which ultimately turns them into a better reality.

On a team-building retreat, a team brainstormed how their company could develop more innovative products to give them a competitive edge in their industry. After rigorous head scratching and formulating a dozen ideas, one team member, who had reached a point of absolute pessimism and was on the verge of giving up, looked at the ideas jotted on the white board, pointed out one and said, "That's *impossible.*" Another teammate, who had stayed positive amidst all the brainstorming when others were starting to think negatively, advised, "Sometimes the reason we can't find our way around problems is often because our own way of thinking is standing in the way. By trying to get our heads around it, we end up moving around in circles. Let's just think it through and get our heads through it. Look at things and this idea differently. Re-read between the lines and view this situation with a more innovative eye. We have an idea that can grow our business if we look at it opportunistically. Conceivably we have labelled this idea *impossible* but it is whispering something of value to us, 'Don't be quick to label me *impossible*, read between the lines with a positive mental attitude because I am saying to you, "*I'm possible*". That's the magic of a positive mental attitude; everything that is labeled *impossible* is in fact saying, '*I'm possible.*'"

"We, in the United Arab Emirates, have no such word as "Impossible"; it does not exist in our lexicon. Such a word is used by the lazy and the weak, who fear challenges and progress. When one doubts their potential and capabilities as well as their confidence, they will lose the compass that leads them to success and excellence, thus failing to achieve their goals. I require you, youth, to insist on number one."

HH Sheik Mohammed Bin Rashid Al Maktoum

PROSPERITY CONSCIOUSNESS

There are two kinds of consciousness in success. The scarcity consciousness is evident in people who make find excuses as opposed to creating ways to achieve their goals . These people hold a set of common beliefs among them that there aren't enough resources and opportunities in this world for them to reach their goals. They settle for less, are happy with where they are, and hardly seek to become more in life. People who have the scarcity consciousness greatly believe that certain things in this world are just too much to have and certain things are meant for certain people. They maintain linear thinking, believing that success comes through hard labour and long hours of restless work and believe that to be successful they must give away everything they have, including their family and friends. The scarcity consciousness is a self-impoverishing way of thinking.

Scarcity thinking gravitates to negative thoughts, scapegoating, complaints, laziness and irresponsibilities. These people expect circumstances out of their control to improve their lives. They blame their circumstances for their situations in life, often deflecting the real problem, which is their attitude to things over which they have no control. A typical person of this mindset often resorts to negative conversations. Their common vocabulary includes limiting phrases such as, it's difficult', it can never happen,' 'I can't do that, that's not meant for people like me,' 'That is just a dream,' or it's impossible.'

Prosperity consciousness is a positive outlook on life. Opportunities and resources are abundant in the eyes of a person with a prosperity consciousness. Their beliefs allow them to approach life youthfully, ignorant of failures, criticism and rejection. They believe they should be fearless in pursuit of their goals and dreams and have cultivated an understanding of life that allows them to pursue their life's aspirations. They believe the most dangerous way to play is to play it safe. To them risk is the new safe. They know that life consists not in the prosperity of things that one possesses but in the consciousness of that what you really are. Starbucks CEO, Howard Schultz, came from a family of modest means but had a prosperity consciousness. In one interview he recounts, "Growing up I always felt like I was living on the other side of the tracks. I knew the people on the other side had more resources, more money, happier families."

People with a prosperity consciousness have a non-linear way of thinking. They know there are no limits to what they can achieve, and they know that success is an obligation, not an option. They believe they cannot settle for less in life. They think of life as an opportunity, not as a burden. They believe that they must give it their best shot and live it to their utmost capacity. People who have tapped into their prosperity consciousness are among the wealthiest people in the world. They are considered to have world-class thinking as opposed to a scarcity consciousness.

In any situation, ask yourself what the opportunity is instead of what the problem is. Instead of being scared by the desert, be inspired by the horizon and walk confidently through the desert to the horizon. Life is just as good as you see it, therefore cultivate the habit of learning more, surrounding yourself with people who empower you and make the possibility of your dreams a reality. Go to good places that inspire you, fascinate your imagination and liberate your spirit. There is a reservoir from which all of us can tap in order to attract our infinite greatness and prosperity, and that reservoir is our prosperity consciousness.

A now successful businessman, who grew up in a shack in the township of Thembisa in South Africa, was sent to a special school for troubled children in high school. He was not considered bright and he made it through school barely passing. While his friends shied away from a life of poverty by stealing and pick pocketing people in the neighbourhood, Billy Selekane caught taxis on weekends to go to OR Tambo Airport to view airplanes take off and disappear gracefully into the sky. He continued this pastime as a hobby he nourished and loved, and deep within him a longing to one day see the world, board a plane, and cross to the other side of the world was gradually growing into a conviction.

Billy went back home in the evenings inspired and motivated to want to be more, achieve more, become more, to leave poverty behind as a wealthy and respectable man in society and the world at large. As he continually invested his thoughts in the possibility of success as a businessman, travelling the world as a global businessman - flying business class - changed the way he thought about himself, his beliefs and, most importantly, his circumstances. He soon cultivated in himself a prosperity consciousness and a realisation that abundance, wealth and good health start from within. A conviction that began as a hobby became a pivotal point that changed the way he thought and still thinks about his potential. He used this mindset change to make positive affirmations that led to productive and different decisions in his life.

While the friends he grew up with were always complaining and blaming their backgrounds and circumstances in life as their limiting factors, Billy made a conscious decision to become a victor of his circumstances instead of a victim. This decision ultimately changed the actions he took in his life. His first action was investing in himself by reading books that expanded and reinforced his newly found beliefs about success. Immersing himself in this learning, he crafted what he concluded was his a grand life vision. This compelling and demanding vision ignited a burning desire in him, eradicating any limiting beliefs and any self-doubt. Continually checking our beliefs is critical because our mind distorts our perception of reality in order to make it conform to our beliefs.

"Abundance is not something we acquire. It is something we tune into."
Dr. Wayne Dyer

Billy's first attempts at small business failed dismally, but he was not discouraged or disempowered. To him failure was not a dead-end, it was a detour, giving him valuable information to be used wisely to make positive future decisions. Thinking through his business failures, dissecting and understanding exactly what he had done wrong and how to fix it to avoid repeating the same mistakes helped Billy turn his life around in less than five years. Today he is a serial entrepreneur, business leader and international business speaker who travels across the world motivating and inspiring people of all genders, races, and backgrounds.

What had changed in this man's life? He did not win the lottery, nor did life hand him aces. He merely changed his belief system. He eradicated the scarcity consciousness of believing that there is not enough for everyone to make a living. He made up his mind that his own way of thinking was the one that was bringing that poverty into his life. He decided the real problem, the only thing stopping him from living the life he rightfully and justly deserved was one thing only, the man in the mirror.

By finding the real problem and accepting it, Billy's perspective changed and he found ways to solve the problem and become a better person, wealthy in life and healthier in mind, body and spirit. The township he grew up in did not change; the people he grew up around did not change; the economy of his country did not change. The only thing that changed was what he believed about himself, what he was capable of and what he was meant to be in the world. A Jewish proverb says that sometimes one must go through the ashes to find one single spark.

The change in Billy opened a completely new world for him and his family, a world of innumerable opportunities and countless possibilities, of endless business and holiday travels across the world and great material and spiritual wealth. Billy's is the story of an individual who walked boldly out of the scarcity consciousness into a prosperity consciousness and it paid off, really paid off. With his humble confidence and mature passion in his work of inspiring others to reach greater heights in their lives; today he owns a mansion in the state of the art Serengeti golf estate in South Africa and his children have a life far better than the one he had growing up in Thembisa township.

Success is when you seek, find and cultivate positive values and principles in your life and use those principles in positive practice to yield positive outcomes and experiences in your life. It is your faith that will guide you and permit you to create the life you have always desired. By all means include other people and establish an environment in which taking a step to realise your dreams also helps others summon enough courage and determination to realise their own. Only when you believe in your own true potential will you begin to witness great things happening in your life.

Let your true self, your true identity and your true light shine. And as you share your gifts , you allow your true light to shine. Everything that is, everything that you are at this point in your life, is a manifestation of your thoughts, whether you are aware of those thoughts or not. Believe in yourself and your power, the power to take control of and direct your life. That power is within you.

The legacy of your life is in your own life story. By creating your story through realising your vision and self-belief, you written your own history. Your vision is the underlying power that makes the difference in your life. Through the actions you take, the steps you take, you write your own history. Every step you take towards your dream means you are writing a page in the book of your history. Prosperity is an open invitation from Nature to everyone. Anyone who wants to be successful is welcome. Just tune into your prosperity consciousness. Give the best of yourself to the world, and the world will give the best of itself to you.

In life you don't go to new places; you discover new possibilities. You will not explore new opportunities in life unless you let go of your own old convictions. Nothing under the sun or within the grasp of the circumference of your imagination is impossible. The nature of Nature itself is prosperity. This reaffirms the notion that you are part of this prosperity and this prosperity is part of you. This is evidence that a life of abundance awaits you.

THE 7 CHAKRAS OF S-U-C-C-Ė-S-S

Abundance, joy, happiness, health, fulfilment and wealth come through self-mastery. To an athlete, success is about breaking records; to engineers, success is about building the best skyscrapers, roads and highways. A prosperity consciousness is what each and every one is born with. Success is not reserved for few individuals, it is a birthright. Each of us was born under a cloud with a silver lining; some of us just decided to hide under a dark cloud of fear. We all have a birthright to succeed in life and we are each responsible to strive for that success. Success is an art in its own way, the realisation of your worthy purpose. As you align these elements in your life, you will radiate boundless life and everything in your life will fall into its place. Achieving success of any sort in life means understanding that you need to have the following in order and in harmony.

SENSE OF PURPOSE – your purpose in life is the voice of your heart, the true song of your soul. It is that one thing that gives you a sense of relevance to this world and gives meaning to why you are alive. As Pablo Picasso says, "The meaning of life is to find your gift. The purpose of life is to give it away." When you find what you love in this world, and love what you do, then find a way of making a living out of it. So that what you do for a living and what you do for fun are one and the same thing. When you are in your element, a point in life where your passion meets your talent, your life becomes a fountain of prosperity, joy, health, wealth and spiritual fulfilment. You become one with your inner self; your creative skills turn everything you do into a work of excellence. Whatever you touch becomes as good as gold. You become an expression of divine love.

UNDERSTANDING – self-knowledge creates self-appreciation and self-appreciation increases self-worth. The more you try to be perfect, the further you actually move away from being perfect. Perfection is self-appreciation. By understanding yourself, you are in a position to better understand life and therefore to direct it towards a fulfilling existence. For most people, the cause of frustration is not knowing who they are. The cure for that frustration is self-understanding.

Life is like an ocean; our souls are streams of life into that ocean. We need to enrich the experience of life for others with our talents, skills and abilities. By not using your gifts to enrich life, then you impoverish the experience of life for others, creating a sense of aimlessness and purposelessness, a life with no direction and meaning. Understand yourself, then make the best out of your true self.

Reaffirm to yourself the understanding that you were born to be great, and the fact that you are here and living now is testimony to that. Take a moment to ponder where you have been and look further to where you are going. By realising that, you have overcome obstacles and achieved a milestone.

CHARITY – we can only grow by growing others. To give respect to all people irrespective of their race, ethnicity, religious beliefs, orientation and any life background is to give yourself the experience of transcending into a world where all material boundaries and walls of the world cease to exist. Stevie Wonder once said, "*Use your heart to love somebody and if your heart is big enough, then use your heart to love everybody.*"

Give of your talents, skills and abilities cheerfully and accept the rewards earned from them as gratefully as you can. Follow your dream with utmost conviction, and consider the rightful ecology of such pursuit, for everything that is done with good intentions returns good rewards to you. As Edwin Markham said, "*There is a destiny that makes us brothers; none goes his way alone. All that we send into the lives of others comes back into our own.*"

COURAGE – the word courage is derived from the old French word, *Corage*, which means heart. Courage therefore means your ability to silence the noises in your head and listen to the voice of your heart. Because only your heart can speak the language of the universe. To live life from the bottom of your heart. To sing the song of your life and dance to its tune while walking boldly in the direction it leads you to. Only your heart knows where you rightfully belong. In whichever way you look at it, your courage moves you forward in life and success is directly or indirectly influenced by your fear of staying behind. People who fear mediocrity strive for greatness. When it comes to pursuing your dreams, there are no risks, only rewards.

A ship is built in the harbour, but it is not meant to stay there, therefore cultivate the habit of courage. Life begins at the end of your comfort zone. Just as the caterpillar thought life was over, it turned into a butterfly; just as the flood ends, the rainbow appears in the sky. Have the courage to let go of the things that are holding you back and hold on to the things that propel you towards your greatness.

EFFICACY – this is a state of absolute contentment with yourself, your abilities and your talents. Self-efficacy is the absence of self-doubt, the knowing of your true self-worth and potential to make whatever you want to achieve possible. When you have a sense of self-efficacy, your awareness of self, of people around you and the resources at your disposal gain a new meaning. You feel adequate, fulfilled and content with whom you really are; you begin to measure yourself against the standards you have set for yourself in life and use your talents and gifts ecologically to make the environment and people around you better in their pursuits.

In Thomas Troward's maxim, "Principle is not bound by precedent. We should not limit our expectations of the future; and if our speculations lead us to the conclusion that we have reached a point where we are not only able, but also required, by law of our own being, to take a more active part in our personal evolution than heretofore, this discovery will afford us a new outlook upon life and widen our horizon with fresh interests and brightening hopes."

To have self-efficacy is to lay a solid foundation where you can exercise and explore your creative confidence and potential without any self-doubt of the outcome of it. Embracing your creative imagination requires efficacy in your abilities and talents. Allow yourself to use them to their optimum; thereby creating a pathway to fully enjoy your life and the richness it holds for you.

SELF-CONFIDENCE – if you do not believe in yourself, the question is who will then believe in you? If you do not believe in your goals, who will believe in them then? Everything starts with you. As you set up your mind about your destiny, you will walk the path with confidence and boldness. Avoid the worn out, beaten paths that have been walked by the multitudes. To make a difference in this world, start first by being different. Take the road that has not been taken before. In one of his poems, Robert Frost advises on the road not travelled as all that makes the difference. Choose your own path, not the one trod by many before you.

Hold yourself in high esteem and set high standards for yourself. Do not measure yourself against other people's standards; measure yourself against the standards you have set for yourself. Deny the naysayers and the skeptics who never had the courage to pursue their dreams to project their self-doubts and insecurities on to you. Ignore all the noises around you that say it's impossible. Listen to the voice inside of you that says you will be the first one to do it, to prove that it is possible and that it can be done.

SELF-ACCEPTANCE – the best you can be and the greatest gift you can give to this world is accepting and expressing your true self. Avoid trying to be like anyone else. Be the best of you because everyone else is already taken. The problem with most people is that they spend so much time trying to be like the next person that they lose out on the great person that's in the mirror.

"You can search throughout the entire universe for someone who is more deserving of your love and affection than yourself, and that person is not to be found anywhere. You, yourself, as much as anybody in the entire universe, deserve your love and affection."

Siddhartha Gautama

In my observations on many people, certain patterns emerged. Many people tend to under price their skills, under value their worth, under estimate their potential and undermine their talents. As a result of this they end up settling for a life that is less than what they are capable of. They end up putting a price tag on their themselves that is less than what they are truly worth. This is self-defeatism, and in an African proverb, "*When there is no enemy within, the enemies outside cannot hurt you.*" When people put themselves in the 'Under-Scale' in everything they are and everything they are capable of, then life helps them settle there.

Michael Jackson's song "Man in the Mirror" evangelises an earnest truth. To make a change in this world, then you need to start with the person in the mirror and change your ways. As you aspire to make a change in this world, start by accepting who you really are and make the best of it. Yesterday you were clever, so you wanted to change the world. Today you are wise, so you are changing yourself.

The best person you can be in this world is yourself; therefore make the best of that person. Your authenticity is your specialty; your awareness of your uniqueness is your blessing. When you come to this self-acceptance, you move into a state of awareness of your potential, talents and abilities. The effort to reach this level of self-awareness means letting go of any preconceived ideas of what is an acceptable identity by people or the environment around you. Recognise that what you feel deeply in your heart and see in your mind, what you know you are supposed to be, you are right, you have always been right about it. That which you seek in your heart is also seeking you. So take a stand and go for it, go, be it.

"*Everyone has been made for some particular work and the desire for that work has been put in every heart.*"

Jalal Al- din Rumi

AMBITION

"Ambition leads to greater fulfilment on an individual basis. As we use our imagination to create new horizons and frontiers for what we can achieve in our lives...."

The most valuable element every individual needs is a certain degree of ambition. Talent requires ambition as a fuel in order to give it meaning and purpose. Ambition leads to greater fulfilment on an individual basis as we use our imagination to create new horizons and frontiers for what we do in our lives. By imagining what we could be and achieve, we move beyond the boundaries we have previously set for ourselves. Ambition therefore has a novelty and also relevance in terms of changing what we do and what we believe about our potential, which is yet to be realised. The saying that the sky is the limit actually means that there are no limits, yet the statement in itself is limiting. The reality is that the only limits we have in life are the ones we impose on ourselves.

The reality is that ambition, for lack of a better word, is great. Ambition is right, ambition works. Ambition clarifies, cuts through and captures the essence of the evolutionary spirit of success. Ambition, in all of its forms — for a better and more fulfilling life, for success, for your dreams and aspirations, ambition to become a better at what you do, a better leader, a better manager, a better person in society, in the organisation. Ambition for more knowledge and more skills has undoubtedly marked the upward surge of where we are today, who we have become and, most importantly, who we will be tomorrow. Ambition is a vehicle for our desired destiny. It will not only save you from your current reality, it will catapult you to greater heights.

We all have one thing in common. It is not our biology, citizenship of a country — it is not anything along those lines. My question to you is what defines you? What makes you different from the person next to you, or from anyone you are thinking about right now? What is it that when you walk out of the door or stand up from the chair you are on right now defines your journey in life?

Most people spend their days looking for excuses to justify why they are where they are right now and why they are not where they want to be in life. Ironically, it requires as much effort and time to look for excuses and circumstances that keep you glued to your comfort zones as it does to find ways and means to be who you want to be and achieve the dreams you have set for yourself.

Many people spend incalculable time looking for and finding reasons why their current circumstances in life are stopping them from achieving their dreams. My question, however, is are your current circumstances in life stopping you or are you using them to stop yourself from reaching your full potential and achieving your dreams?

It is my conviction, for everyone, that; '*Whatever the height of imagination and dreams your mind can reach, then the depth of your courage and capabilities can manifest.*' This is irrespective of your race, ethnicity, background, religion or any conventional limitation known to man. My advice to you is simple. If only you practise the mental discipline of focusing your mind and heart to your dreams and aspirations and concentrating all your actions in that direction, then you will become absolutely unstoppable. Whatever situation you are in right now, it's your finest opportunity; it's what you have, so make the best of it because it is not what you have but what you make out of what you have that makes a difference.

"People are always blaming their circumstances for what they are. I don't believe in circumstances. The people who get on in this world are the people who get up and look for the circumstances they want, and, if they can't find them, make them."

George Bernard Shaw

It is not your current circumstance, it is your current attitude towards your circumstances in life that will determine the altitude of your success. To make a difference you start by being different. That is the only difference that makes the difference. While everyone is busy living their fears, be busy finding ways to live your dreams.

Take a moment to breathe, take a break from complaining and take time to count your blessings. To your amazement you will realise that they outnumber your problems. Be grateful enough to realise that you are not better than anybody and wise enough to realise that you are different from the rest. Your dream is your identity, therefore hold on to it. Keep the fire in you to make it come true alive. That is the only thing you really have in this world that no one can take away from you.

The key thing is to lay a concrete foundation for your ambitions of four fundamentals. By having these four fundamentals intact, you have success in your hands. The fundamentals are:

GOALS - Have a definite goal of the things you want to be achieve, a vision of the things you want to have tomorrow. Having a vision of the life you want.

MANAGE YOUR STATE - Striking a balance in your state of emotions and, more importantly, your state of mind guides you to achieve your desired outcome. A negative attitude towards people, your circumstances, obstacles, and challenges will lead you to mediocrity. Mediocrity is tailor made for people who don't have the right attitude.

EMPOWERING BELIEFS - As you focus yourself on the feelings of gratitude and memories of things you succeeded in, you evoke in yourself empowering beliefs.

STRATEGY - The truth is whether you believe you can or believe you can't, whichever belief you stick to, you will end up being right. By developing viable short-term, medium-term and long-term strategy, you find ways to organise and utilise your resources optimally. By believing in your goals and ambitions, then your life must depend on them and devise a strategy to see them realised.

"It is the duty of ambition to drive, and it is your duty to keep ambition alive and driving."
Robert Collier

In pursuit of your goals, cultivate a sense of urgency; '*What can be done tomorrow must be done today, what can be done today must be done now and what can be done now should have been done yesterday.*' This sense of urgency must be the ultimate driving force in you to charge boldly towards your dreams to tap into your infinite potential and unlock countless possibilities for yourself. Ask yourself whether you see far in life because you are standing on a giant's shoulder or is it because you are a giant yourself. Soon you will realise that you are a giant yourself.

By all means, and whichever way we look at it, ambition is a guiding light, it sets the precedence for providence, for what you can achieve and be, and it brings the best out of you. It clarifies the path you need to take in life to reach your destiny; it cuts through all odds. Ambition, in all of its forms, to have a better life, to achieve more, to do more and reach your utmost potential, has undoubtedly driven everyone who has achieved his dreams. The powerful force of ambition has for centuries marked the upward surge of civilisation. As Quintus Horatius Flaccus said, "*Nothing is too high for the daring of mortals: we would storm it in our folly.*"

To succeed, set high standards for yourself. Rules are merely commonly acceptable standards of excellence. Success begins when you set higher standards for yourself than the ones commonly accepted. Do not limit yourself to your current circumstances or your environment. Some people see and experience the burden of life while some people choose to see and experience the beauty of life. Whichever way you look at it, your perceptions about life are entirely dependent upon you.

The question, however, is how much are you willing to work hard, to sacrifice and to pursue your ambition. People say they are afraid of failure; how much then do they fear to live the life they never aspired to live because they fear taking action? Do you fear your success or do you fear your failure? By not pursuing your ambitions in life you are then in fact pursuing your failures — failure to achieve the goals you have set for yourself and failure to live the life you aspire for and deserve to live. What exactly is stopping you? Nothing.

The interesting part is realising that the only difference between where you are supposed to be and where you are right now is usually the result of your internal dialogue, stories you tell yourself about your dreams not working out. How will you know if you don't try, how will you ever know if you don't take the first step? Already by not taking the first step, you have failed to realise your ambitions. Would you rather you fear this way, where it impedes your life, or would you rather fear mediocrity and take the first step out of it into your true greatness?

Not being happy about the way things are in your life or the way the world is, sitting down and moaning and groaning solves nothing, makes everything worse than it already is. The answer is to be solution focused instead of problem focused. Stand up and do something about the circumstances you need to be happy. If the circumstance cannot be changed, then the attitude towards it can be changed. To make a positive change in your life, then you need to start first by changing the person in the mirror. The problem with most people is that they are too busy trying to look like the next person that they lose on the great person in the mirror.

All that you are right now and all that you will ever be is entirely dependent upon your state of mind. Your beliefs about yourself and your place in this world are arguably the prime determinant of your success. You actually have more to give to this world than you can take from it. So all you need to do is to stand up and give it your best shot. You can either take punches from life, get beaten down to the point where you don't know what to do with your life, or you can give it your best shot and become the person you are supposed to be. When it comes to thinking ahead and being ahead in life, you don't need anyone to do that for you; you just need to look into the beauty of your future and carve your own destiny.

"I want to be around people that do things. I don't want to be around people any more that judge or talk about what people do. I want to be around people who dream. And support. And do things."

Amy Poehler

First thing first, stay away from negative people; they will bring out the worst in you instead of bringing out the best in you. They are like weeds to your ambitions and dreams, they are poison that will kill your dreams and stop them from blossoming into reality. Be realistic enough to recognise that old habits will not yield new outcomes in your life, they will not open new doors and possibilities in your life. They will shut all the doors of a better life on you. Be ignorant of what you are incapable of and aware of your capabilities. Have no boundaries or limitations because your world is what you make of it. What you dare to dream, dare to do and dare to be with all force, might and no iota of doubt.

Rome was not built in a day. Equally true, Dubai was not built overnight. It took five hundred years to get the Duomo in Milan where it is today. Not that it will take you five hundred years to build your dream, but it certainly won't be an overnight thing. One step at a time, one achievement at a time, one milestone at a time and eventually the mist will clear. The road will become smoother and the destiny clearer in your eyes by your dedicating yourself wholeheartedly to the achievement of your ambitions. It is not necessary to lower your ambitions and standards to make those around you feel less intimidated. Why try to fit in when you were born to stand out? Your authenticity in your individuality is what makes you distinguishable; it separates you from the rest and makes you the best. Rather look back and say, "*I can't believe I did that,*" than look back and say, "*Why didn't I do that?*" Take responsibility for your life and ambitions because no one is going to jump in the ring of life, take punches for you and then hand *you* the gold medal.

"Be yourself; everybody else is already taken."
Oscar Wilde

Embrace the reality that what lies behind you and what lies ahead of you is nothing compared to the greatness that lies within you. Your greatness is embodied in your thoughts about your potential and your belief in your destiny. When you know better, you do better; when you do better, you become better. The possibilities available to you in your life are relative to your capabilities. When you begin to explore your capabilities, you open a door to greater possibilities for your life.

One of the most inspiring stories on ambition and how it can lead to success is that of Cesar Ritz, the founder of the Swiss hotel chain, the Ritz Hotel Development Company. Cesar was born in 1850 in the small Swiss village of Niederwald. The youngest of thirteen children in a poor family, he began his career as a waiter in restaurants in Paris, and then moved to work in some high-class restaurants. Here he served some of the city's wealthiest people, who were an inspiration to him. Later he worked as a hotel manager. Through serving wealthy clients, he cultivated a rich sense of life and a taste for elegant things, which would be the foundation of his later successful move to hotel developer.

Ritz's attitude in life was that his work as a waiter was not an end in his life; rather it was a means to an end. He saw his job as a necessary part of his life that would cultivate in him the necessary skills and principles to eventually one day run his own hotels. In his interviews he explains his attitude throughout his career as a waiter until he became a wealthy hotel chain owner:

"I never saw myself as a salesman, whatever I happened to be selling on the telephone or door-to-door. I always saw myself as the guy who was going to run this place one day, or run some sort of organisation like it." Instead of seeing himself as running the organisation for someone else, he saw himself as the owner. He accepted where he was as a necessary place he had to be in order to learn what he had to learn and do what he had to do to get to the next higher level.

"I was always looking for opportunities for leadership, for opportunities to contribute, for ways to develop relationships with higher-ups who could help me and whom I could help. My peers typically were not my co-workers. I was not the guy who hung around the coffee pot with everyone else. I was the guy who came in an hour earlier than everyone else. I was friendly, but I was not going to work for camaraderie with my co-workers.

"I cared. They saw it just as a lousy job that got them to Friday. I saw it as a necessary step to get me from being the guy doing the 'lousy job' to the guy that's running the operation that provides all these jobs, and then to the guy that owns the business that provides all the jobs. I never thought of them as lousy at any step of the way. I always thought of them as very worthy, and very much a part of the process.

"When I became the manager and then the owner of these types of businesses, I tried to encourage my employees to view things this way, so they could rise through the ranks of the company. But very few ears were ready to hear that. Most people saw their jobs from a short-term perspective. They were not thinking the long game. When you are thinking just in terms of this month or the next six months, it makes sense to see your job as just a lousy source of a pay cheque. But not when you are thinking about the next ten years."

"It is better to be prepared for an opportunity and not have one than to have an opportunity and not be prepared."
Whitney M. Young

A valuable lesson from Ritz Carlton's story we can learn is simple; *think big, think long term, stay sharp and keep focused.* Each of us should be honest with ourselves and set realistic goals in our lives and stop hoping for miracles to happen. Cultivate a sense of ambition. Never surrender despite the challenges you face daily. The examples in this book show that success can be simple when an individual has the basic elements of personal character and aspiration, with a bit of luck thrown in. Life has no bad experiences, but some people just have bad attitudes.

"Twenty years from now you will be more disappointed by the things that you didn't do than by the ones you did do. So throw off the bow lines. Sail away from the safe harbour. Catch the trade winds in your sails. Explore. Dream. Discover."
H. Jackson Brown, Jr

When inspiration does not propel you to your dreams, then resort to desperation. Your dreams are the keys to the liberation of your true self, your true potential and greatness. The world will only open up its abundance to you when you open up the abundance within you to it. The magnitude of your ambition is relative to the scale of your imagination and proportional to the depths of your courage.

AMBITION ACCELERATION CYCLE

Behavioural psychology has proven that what goes into your mind is usually reflected by the actions you take in your life. Your potential is not limited by birth or anything else but by your own belief about your capability. People who are successful in life have one thing in common; they have supernatural beliefs about themselves and what they can achieve. They believe that they can achieve whatever goals they set for themselves in their lives and then go on to take actions to achieve those goals.

This does not make them unique or gifted in any way; they just understand the power of their thinking. Your brain is compacted energy, it constantly vibrates, releasing energy into the universe. Your thoughts are the frequency that gets released into the universe and informs the universe, which then conspires to fulfilling them. Your mind sends out this frequency through your thoughts and then your intuition guides you on how to take action that brings you closer to your desired outcome. This process can be conscious or subconscious.

For the past millennia, a multitude of people whose deeds have filled the pages of our history books had one thing in common. Each of them understood and embraced the power of their thoughts. They knew that their imagination was a powerful force that shaped their future. They understood that a thought is a source of creation, that by merely concentrating their thoughts on something, they had already given it power to manifest into reality.

Everyone is entirely responsible and accountable for the reality they have created for themselves in their lives. This is because reality is a manifestation of the sum total of thoughts, beliefs, decisions and actions. In trying to understand what makes people do what they do, or become what they want to be, let's look at the Ambition Acceleration Model derived from behavioural learning theory, TOTE model.

Thoughts are living things. In the Thought phase of the model, your thought is the trigger of the chain reaction of actions that you will take and the outcomes you will experience. This thought can be from

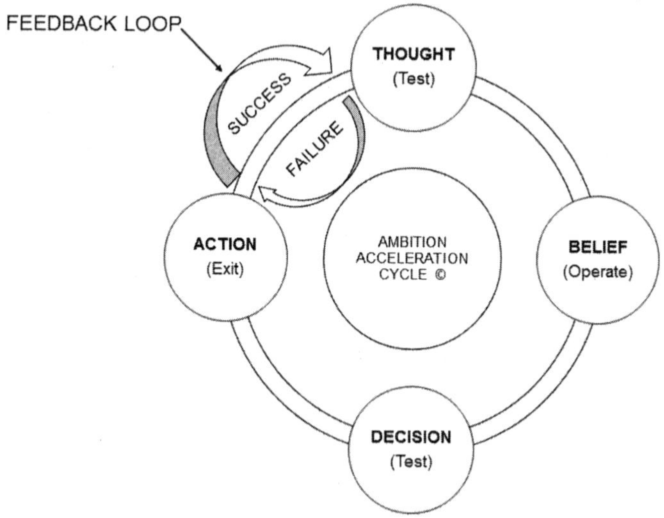

an external or internal source, meaning you could have picked it up externally from your environment, friends, media or internally from within you, your own inner thoughts.

A thought you entertain in your mind, whether negative or positive, is empowered by how you much you nurture it. Let's explore this process. You create or conceive a thought and then transform it by playing it in your mind or thinking it through. Once you have thought it through, you test its desirability, feasibility and viability. By taking it through this brief test, you accept it and then you filter it into the next phase. Any thought held long enough in the mind is like wealth invested in valuable shares — it grows.

"Nurture your mind with great thoughts, for you will never go any higher than you think."
Benjamin Disraeli

In the '*Belief*' phase of this cycle, the thought is transformed into a *belief*. You know you can be the best team player, manager, president or

CEO of a company. By pondering over it long and hard enough you start believing in it. As Mohammed Ali once said, "*It is the repetition of affirmations that leads us to a certain belief, and once that belief becomes a deep conviction with us, then great things begin to happen.*"

When you have moulded the thought in your mind long enough, it becomes a conviction. It now operates in your belief system and once a positive thought operates in your belief system, it will expand the depth of your potential, or at least your belief in what you are capable of achieving. Whatever you believe you can achieve or cannot achieve, either way you are always right. Beliefs are like compounding interest; they lever your thoughts. Negative beliefs will cost you a fortune and your health. Your belief system is a fertile garden, where the seeds of your thoughts will grow. Therefore sow positive and empowering thoughts in your mind. The strategy is to compound positive beliefs. Once you operate on positive beliefs, then you move into the third phase of the Ambition Acceleration Cycle, the 'Decision' phase.

"Compound interest is the eighth wonder of the world. He, who understands it earns it ... he who doesn't ... pays it."
Albert Einstein

In this phase, as you consolidate your beliefs about your thoughts, about your convictions and evoke an inner sense of compelling edge to decide upon the belief and finding a way of acting upon it, you seek evidence to support your decision, then build a strategy or road map for executing the decision. A decision naturally has a redemptive power to shape your destiny and give a new meaning to your journey.

In beliefs, you seek internal and external evidence to reinforce the decision, to conclude that it is the right decision to take based upon your beliefs about what you can do and achieve. As you start off with a positive thought, it will have transformed into a positive belief system. When you started off with a negative thought, it will contaminate your belief system and convince you that you are capable of achieving less.

"It is in our moment of decision that our destiny is shaped."
Tony Robbins

As you think more of your potential, you make decisions that support your thoughts. By thinking highly of yourself and your potential, you naturally make positive decisions and take big conclusions about what you can do, be and achieve. Your decisions in life are shaped by your beliefs about yourself and what you are capable of achieving. Empowering beliefs, inspire you to take empowering actions all the time. After concretising your belief system, and your decisions concluded, you enter the last and most important phase, the Action phase, shaping your decisions into visible and tangible form.

Your actions are the realisation of your thoughts. What you do and what you become echo your state of the mind and the thoughts that simmer into your mind. Successful people take big actions, they have big beliefs. They think big and make big decisions. In the end they achieve big things in their lives. Action is a courageous thought manifested in reality. Any thought is just as powerful as the actions that back it up. When you think positively in life, when you believe in yourself and in your goals, you make decisions that guide you towards achieving those goals. The actions you take, the steps you make, are defining moments in your life. Life is a huge repository of experiences and moments; pick only the fulfilling and meaningful experiences in your life, which will then harness your positive attitude.

Positive attitude yields positive outcomes; a greater attitude catapults you into even higher altitudes in your life. This will further widen the magnitude of your success and increase your gratitude for greater achievements in life.

The Ambition Acceleration Cycle guides you in understanding the power of your thoughts. How to direct what goes into your mind, how it can influence your thoughts, affect the decisions you make and dictate the actions you take; which ultimately leads to the results you will achieve and your results shape your reality. The greatest power you have is the power to take control of your own mind and your thoughts and direct them to the ends and means you desire. Never allow negative thoughts to contaminate your belief system. This will rob you of achieving your goals and realising your potential.

"The greatest danger for most of us is not that our aim is too high and we miss it, but that it is too low and we reach it."

Michelangelo

THE MOMENT OF TRUTH - WHAT IS REALLY STOPPING YOU

If you are not where you want to be at the moment, it is simply because you have not yet taken a stand, stood up and walked towards the place you want to be. Perhaps you have spent so much time nourishing your self-doubts that you start believing in them. You are either a victim or a victor of your fears in this world. Whichever way you perceive it, the ball is in your court. Are your fears holding you back or are you using your fears to hold yourself back? Ponder this question long enough and you will realise that your fears have no power over you except the power you give them by believing them to be true. Whatever you fear is just an illusion. More often that which you fear is not your monster, your beliefs in your fears are the monsters.

Controlling your life with your fears means you can also use those same fears to alter your attitude towards your circumstances and yourself. Nothing stops you in this world but you. It is only when you decide to reveal the blessings and abundance within you to the world that the world will reveal its abundance. You have all that you need already, but to access it requires you to tap into the resourcefulness within you to reach for your dreams.

Instead of complaining about situations find reasons to complement them. Stop looking for reasons why you can't achieve your goals and start looking for ways of achieving them. Discard thoughts that hold you back. Embrace thoughts that inspire you, that compel you to reach out for more in life, be more, achieve more and experience more success in your life and allow your intuition to safely guide you in achieving them. Trust your first instincts; they have good intentions for you. Ignore your second thoughts about yourself; they ignite self-doubt. Want it? Then go for it. Second thoughts are designed to kill the killer instinct in you. They fuel self-doubt and self-questioning, which ultimately lead to self-destruction and more fears.

"The question isn't who is going to let me; it's who is going to stop me."
Ayn Rand

Let go of the things that hold you back and hold on to the things that empower you to charge boldly towards your dreams. Your ambitions, your positive thoughts, your memorable experiences and moments of victories are the resources you should tap into within you to ignite your resourcefulness and propel you into the reality of your dreams. Reach out for the stars; it is only when you reach out for them that they will reach out for you. Take giant leaps, you are a giant yourself after all, so embrace your greatness, unleash your infinite potential and unlock infinite opportunities and possibilities in your life. You have it, you were born with it. It is your chance now to make the best out of it. You are here and here now because it is your chance to bring out the greatness in you, to bring it out to the world. You have the power in you to make everything you dream of possible. Reach within you for that power. Feel it, see it, hold it and unleash it. What is really stopping you? Nothing at all.

THE PROCESS OF CHANGING YOUR STATE OF MIND

To discover which mindset you are currently in, you need to understand what a mindset is. The difference between a successful person and an unsuccessful person is not dependent upon their biological or physiological state so much as their state of mind. Your response to experiences in your life usually gives an indication of your default mindset.

The brain contains the intangible, the mind, described as the set of cognitive faculties that enables consciousness, perception, thinking, judgement, and memory. The mind has two divisions, the negative mindset and the positive mindset. The negative mindset houses all the undesired ideals and notions that cloud your interpretation of experiences in life. Thus, the positive mindset is an arsenal for all the positive ideals and notions that enrich your experience of life.

Everyone has a default mindset, the state of the mind they use most often. A negative default mindset makes interpretation of experiences in life often self-destructive. You see limits instead of boundaries around you, and you see challenges more often than opportunities. A negative mindset filters out all positive experiences and only focuses on negative experiences. It looks for the bad and deletes any good. A positive mindset creates the best interpretation of experiences in your environment. That is all it looks for and sees in the environment, experiences that enrich your perception of the reality of the world.

To assess what your current default mindset is, ask yourself which words you most often use to describe any experience, past or current. Do you often use words or phrases like, '*I can*'t,' '*It is difficult,*' '*I don't like it,*' '*It is not meant for me,*' '*I don't think I will make it*'? If most of your words are inhibiting words, then your default mindset may be negative. Consciously decide to change this interpretation of your experiences in life. Look out for the best in a situation, a valuable lesson, an important learning curve, and a moment of self-reflection and future projection. Be aware of your gradual shift from a negative mindset and make a positive mindset your default mindset.

In the countryside in Anangu, in the Northern Territory of Australia an old wise man called Tamminya told his grandchildren great stories about life lessons he learnt from his ancestors. The life of the village and battles with other tribes. One night as the old man and his grandchildren sat around the fire, he told them a story of a battle each and every human fights and yet the victory is entirely dependent upon them. He gently uttered, "My lovely children, there is a battle that goes on inside people. The battle is between two beasts inside us. One beast is evil; it symbolises anger, envy, jealousy, sorrow, regret, greed, arrogance, laziness, and guilt, lies, resentment, self-pity and false pride. The other beast is good; it symbolises joy, empathy, generosity, truth, love, peace and compassion." One of his grandsons eagerly asked, "Grandpa, in this ferocious fight, which beast actually wins?" The old man sighed. "The one that you feed every day."

According to a research in neuroscience, the average human being has approximately seventy thousand thoughts a day. This means innumerable interpretations of various experiences in our daily lives. What is critical is to be aware of your ability to choose to ensure that at least a substantial portion of those thoughts are positive. Remember, your perception of the reality you are living at the moment is not a true reflection of reality but rather a reflection of your state of mind, which is merely your mental blueprint of your perception of life and that blueprint is projected by you on the environment around you.

A positive mindset will project only positive interpretation of the experiences in your environment, filtering out all negative ones and focusing you on ones that positively enrich your experience of life. A positive mindset does not see limits, it only sees boundaries, and it does not see challenges but only opportunities wherever it looks. A positive mindset searches for solutions instead of problems; a negative mindset seeks the opposite. Stinking thinking is what I call extremely toxic thoughts. Being positive at all times, regardless of any circumstances, even those that seem insurmountable, also helps you tap into your creative thinking, which helps you find solutions and identify rewarding decisions and actions.

A positive mindset is the gateway to a meaningful and fulfilling life. Constantly cultivating positivity will change your perception of the world. Since your reality is entirely dependent upon your perception of it, you can create a reality that is more desirable, rewarding and meaningful to you. This will be reflected in the thoughts you have, the decisions you make and the actions you take. Regardless of an outcome you desired from your actions, your state of mind will not be adversely affected as you will perceive it as constructive feedback, guiding you to more informed and constructive actions in future. Continuously working on this shift and noticing the results will help you notice your own transformation and be more aware of your state of mind and any actions required whenever you go out of the desired state.

By working harder on your state of mind every day, channelling your thoughts positively by viewing and approaching any circumstance or experience as a guide to the right path, in the right direction for the life you desire, this will help optimise your resources, recognise opportunities and be in a good state to create solutions. When push comes to shove, people with a positive state of mind will take the shovel and dig for a golden opportunity. Their positive mindset is a tool they use to turn any crisis in their lives into an opportunity. They believe that the grass is not necessarily greener on the other side, but it will always be greener where you water it.

PASSION AND DESIRE

"The heart has the natural power to pull the mind into what it is working on. Put your heart where your passion is and the mind will make it happen."

Passion is an essential ingredient that fuels your drive to achieve your goals. Passion empowers your ambitions and makes them more compelling and worth achieving. When people display a passion in something they do, it always seems there is nothing that can stand in their way, even if they seem not to have the means to pursue their aspirations. The presence of passion and desire to bring their dreams into reality ignites a fierce resilience, a *'nothing can stand in my way'* attitude,' so much so that even in the face of what may be a challenge, they find a way around it or turn it into a golden opportunity. Passion is a kind of road map, a guiding light, a pillar of strength, and when you ignite your ambitions with it, the only option at the end of the day is to achieve your dreams.

Many people claim a desire to achieve something; however, that flaming passion is missing from their eyes, the flame that says I am going to get it no matter what it takes. Enthusiasm is the spark that charges you; by its true origin the word 'enthusiasm' comes from the Greek word *enthousiasmos,* which loosely translated means '*to be inspired*'. Some people want to achieve certain things in life, but they never seem to immerse their whole heart, mind, soul and energy into achieving them. Because of that, they never become what they want to be, they never achieve what they want to achieve. They lack passion; the iron fist that can break any wall that is creating a false barrier to your dream.

Some people are so passionate about what they do that they always seem to achieve more. The more passion that feeds their energy, the more they achieve goals they have set for themselves. Passion is the magic that focuses you on your goal. The more passion you have every day, the more successful you are in your work, your job or hobby. I have seen some people who were so passionate about their job that; I swear even if they did not get paid for it, they would still put 150% effort into it. It is what keeps them going, it is what defines them, and it is what they were born to do. In their job they seem to be in touch with their true element and they seem to succeed and flourish easily in life.

Passion is emotion in motion, a catalyst of contagion. An energising and empowering great feeling you get when the mere idea or thought of achieving a goal haunts your mind. You get a shiver down your spine, butterfly sensations in your stomach, a wild heartbeat and every vein in your body is as if electrified. You feel a fuzzy tickle at the tip of your fingers, every hair on your skin stands on end, every muscle subtly twitches, and every cell in your body vibrates to the thought of your passion. It occupies all the faculties of your mind and you can no longer imagine life or live life without it. When you feel this way about your dreams and goals, you are passionate about them and will do whatever you can to achieve them. Passion is the only force that turns the impossible into the possible.

People who love what they do make their mark and succeed because they are a success themselves. They strive to achieve and desire to be the best at what they do because they are passionate about it. They are bound to succeed because they are passionate, which is basically having a positive mental attitude and drive towards their job or anything else they do. Anything approached with a positive attitude and every task done with passion is bound to be well done. Everyone who does anything with passion is bound to achieve the heights and magnitude of success.

Igniting whatever you do with passion always yields not only positive results but success as well. Passion is the magic that is like music in your heart. When you live with it, the flow of ideas, the creativity in your soul spirals to astounding proportions. Many people who have achieved success in their respective fields credit it to the burning passion they feel.

Howard Schultz, the founder of Starbucks, the largest coffee chain restaurant in the world, is driven by one thing — insatiable passion. He admits that he not only enjoys coffee, but he is passionate about it. His passion about serving the world the best coffee is something that has infected his investors, customers, employees and the world at large. The story of Howard Schultz and the founding of Starbucks is fascinating. On vacation in Milan, he stopped by a coffee shop to get a little caffeine refresh. This cup of espresso with steamed milk ignited his passion for mocha frappuccino, a taste that he would take back to the United States. His passion for the taste of coffee saw the American people and eventually the world begin a love affair with Starbucks.

Today, Howard Schultz is a household brand and resident billionaire of the Forbes' list of wealthiest people in the world. Where did it start? With his passion for Italian coffee and a conviction that he had to share this passion with everyone in the world. Passion has made all the difference in his life and the people who have invested in and work for Starbucks.

The term 'p*assion*' encapsulates a powerful meaning. According to the dictionary, the word 'passion' means any powerful or compelling emotion or feeling of doing something. It is this feeling that makes people move mountains, achieve what appears to others as wild dreams. Courage backed by passion is the greatest route to success. Passion is by its simplest definition divine possession. It is my belief that behind passionate people you will find a high power working diligently and tenaciously to express itself through marvelous works, speeches or ideas. Passion is simply being in your element, on a high intellectual plane where you are one with your dream and part of its reality.

In 2012 on the America's Got Talent show, Jessica Sanchez stirred the audience with her finale compilation. The passion in her face while singing Celine Dion's 'The Prague' left even the macho men of this world cuddling with pillows and craving a white chocolate bar. Apart from her beautiful face and melodic voice, Jessica's passion filled her with the magic that ignited a fire in the audience, taking us away from this planet to an imaginary wonder world where each of us would like to go to hoping never to come back.

Jessica's voice seemed to overflow with immeasurable passion, giving to the song everything she had. Of course that passion pouring into the hearts of the audience members inspired endless applause; Jessica's ability to inject her voice with passion energised, inspired, uplifted and empowered the spirits of more than 40 million viewers. Some, including me, couldn't get enough of her rendition of *'I will always love you,'* a song sung by country western singer Dolly Parton and made famous by Whitney Houston. Jessica's version was so amazing it sent many to tears.

"*Every great dream begins with a dreamer. Always remember, you have within you the strength, the patience, and the passion to reach for the stars to change the world.*"
Harriet Tubman

Passion has the power to stir a soul to the point where the passion itself takes complete control and spreads itself on to the next person, until a contagion of endless passionate energy looms in the room. All successful people know the value of leading and living with passion. Richard Branson is well into his sixties, an age at which most people pack their corporate bags to enjoy retirement. But this high-energised entrepreneur always looks as though he just tasted this thing called passion and wants to squeeze the juice out of it.

Having founded the Virgin Group in the early seventies and scraping through by running a mail order business; later a music empire; and now airlines and many other businesses, Branson's passion for his business is only surpassed by a three-year-old toddler's desire to wear Superman's gear and save the world. His burning love for new challenges and ideas, the passion he oozes in his talks, his business and everything he does — all have inspired many other entrepreneurs around the world, including young people and others who are passionate about life.

Passion is undoubtedly a magic spell that stirs a soul to go an extra mile, to explore and reach out for greater heights. It is the fuel that propels anyone to charge forward, to take any challenge by the horns and arm wrestle whatever predicament stands in the way of reaching for a dream. In anything that a person does, when passion is injected, history is often made. Sometimes watching a team of cheerleaders playing with their pom poms and gliding in the air like saints is the greatest display of passion. What even outshines the passion is the wide smiles decorating their faces. This is the greatest form of cheering the crowds, energising them, pumping them up and keeping their spirits high and raging like an inferno.

This way of getting passion to the fans is ultimately passed on to the team after half time, with the coach also casting spells of passion on the team in the changing room. In the movie, *'Any Given Sunday'* Al Pacino, as a coach, gives the most inspirational speech a team could get from their coach. The passion, fire and emotion in him moves souls from their little comfort zones where everything looks impossible to a completely new dimension where even flying is only a flap of hands not requiring wings:

"I don't know what to say really. Three minutes to the biggest battle of our professional lives all comes down to today. Either we heal as a team or we are going to crumble. Inch by inch, play by play till we're finished. We are in darkness right now, gentlemen, believe me, and we can stay here and get defeated or we can fight our way back into the light. We can climb out of this darkness. One inch at a time. Now I can't do it for you. I'm too old. I look around and I see these young faces and I think I mean I made every wrong choice a middle-aged man could make. I uh.... I spent all

my money believe it or not. I chased off anyone who has ever loved me. And lately I can't even stand the face I see in the mirror. You know when you get old in life things get taken from you. That's - that's part of life.

But you only learn that when you start losing stuff. You find out that life is just a game of inches. So is football. Because in either game or life or football the margin for error is so small, I mean one half step too late or too early and you don't quite make it. One half second too slow or too fast and you don't quite catch it. The inches we need are everywhere around us. They are in every break of the game every minute, every second.

On this team we fight for that inch. On this team we tear ourselves and everyone around us to pieces for that inch. We CLAW with our fingernails for that inch. 'Cause we know when we add up all those inches that's going to make the difference between WINNING and LOSING, between LIVING and DYING.

I'll tell you this. In any fight it is the guy who is willing to die who is going to win that inch. And I know if I am going to have any life any more it is because I am still willing to fight and die for that inch because that is what LIVING is. The six inches in front of your face. Now I can't make you do it. You got to look at the guy next to you. Look into his eyes. Now I think you are going to see a guy who will go that inch with you. You are going to see a guy who will sacrifice himself for this team because he knows when it comes down to it, you are going to do the same thing for him.

That's a team, gentlemen, and either we heal now, as a team, or we will die as individuals. That's football, guys. That's all it is. Now, what ya gonna do?"

This speech is one of the most electrifying I have listened to, so much that sometimes even in my sleep I hear Al Pacino standing beside my bed and saying it to me, with the same energy, verve and passion. If I were a football player I would probably be enjoying mega brand endorsements by now. When this dose of passion is injected in an individual, all limiting beliefs, self-doubt and fear are turned to courage, will and excitement to do what may keep an audience's eyes popped out, mouths wide open with surprise, and gripping their chairs as though they had been shocked out of their brains.

Passion is a critical ingredient in driving us to putting our potential to the test, putting ourselves under demanding and liberating situations that force us to tap into our unlimited potential and stretch to reach places and achievements that will be remembered even centuries later when we are merely a memory to the world. By cultivating passion in whatever we set our mind and hearts to achieve, we build a bridge to cross over all things that would set us back on the journey of exploring who we really are and what we are capable of achieving.

Passion is that music playing deep in the chambers of the soul like a symphony, a chord, that when played often, creates a harmonising tone between the universe and the possessor of this miraculous force. Everything that is done with passion is always remarkable, everyone who does whatever task with passion encounters boundless success. Passion liberates the spirit of greatness in us; it cuts through and breaks all possible boundaries. It is that catapult that throws us into the wonderful unknown, the imaginary reality, the beauty of the invisible, and it is the spirit of creation of what is beautiful.

"There is no passion to be found playing small — in settling for a life that is less than the one you are capable of living."
Nelson Mandela

Those who have followed their purpose in life, their dream, what makes them tick, what lights up the fire in them, have been fuelled by immeasurable passion. People driven by passion in whatever they do are resilient, tenacious and relentless. Passionate people all have one thing in common; they understand that the only power that exists to bring their dreams into reality is the passion they bring to them. Fear does not stop them, instead they use it as a fuel for their courage, and they know that their courage to move forward, to walk boldly in the direction of their dreams, is fuelled by their fear of staying behind.

When you do things with passion, you resonate determination, enthusiasm and curiosity, ingredients that when balanced properly yield no doubt, only positive outcomes and insurmountable success. When you commit yourself to a course, give it your all. As you think about it, then think it through, and when you go into it, then go all the way into it. Fear is merely creative imagination used negatively to yield negative outcomes. By virtue of the powers of your imagination, you create your reality.

When you soak your heart and mind into that which you are passionate about, boundless energy and creativity are exuded from within you. Days seem to move faster than hours, hours fade away faster than minutes and minutes go by quicker than seconds. Time and space become one, no beginning, no end, when you are in your element. Passion is the fire that melts steel. It is your burning torch, it is your guiding light, and it is your David's catapult. Channel it into a course that gives more meaning, reward and satisfaction to your life. History has taught us through a multitude of its examples that people whose achievements and inspiring efforts have enriched our history books all had one thing in common - they lived with passion.

"I get to rock the house like Springsteen or Jagger — even though I clearly cannot sing, AND my concerts are 50 hours long! The energy and power of a stadium filled with anticipation is where I go to work every day, that's my office. It may not be a baseball diamond but I'm on the field every day."

Tony Robbins

THINK WAY BEYOND THE BOX

"A playful mind is a creative mind, a creative mind is an intelligent mind, just keep it playing...."

It is great to think. '*Thinking is an art, perfected through practice, mastered by a few; it is simply a weaving of thoughts into beautiful patterns called ideas.*' And ideas are seeds that germinate into value; they are the currency of success. Thomas Edison's idea of the light bulb has not only changed but also illuminated the world. Nobel Prize winner Dr. Arnold Schultz once said, "The problem with people these days is that they don't want to think."

The greatest achievers in the world are the greatest thinkers in the world. They dream by night and by day as well. They come up with brilliant ideas, they solve difficult problems, making life easier for those who do not enjoy dreaming. Hence they are the most successful people in the world. They know that thinking is a sport. If they appreciate and practise it, they will be so good at it that ideas will flow naturally. And ideas are the greatest magnets of success.

Many people lose their creative confidence early in school due to one perpetuated misconception. Often in class kids will give answers to a teacher's question and the answer would be, 'You're wrong, Tom, think out of the box.' Growing older I have concluded that that is often a dangerous thing an intelligent adult can say to a child, because the moment a person tells you to think out of the box, the first thing you think is your answers are not intelligent enough.

As we grow older, this creates a continually self-reinforcing belief that we are not creative nor intelligent, resulting in a depreciating creative confidence as we become adults. The question: is what box? When it comes to thinking there is no box. There are no limits to what we can think, there are no limits to intelligence. We can think whatever we want to think and every thought that comes out of our minds has a chance to change the world for the better.

As we use our intellectual talents to their optimum, we can develop ideas on how to solve problems, create better methods and tools to use when doing our jobs to make them easier, faster and more efficient. Think how we can grow, contribute meaningfully and creatively, so that we can enrich others and our own lives. A friend once said to me while we were at varsity, "We have to be of some service to our fellow human beings to earn a living. The service we render to our fellow others is the rent we pay for our living here on earth."

We don't make money; only the Mint makes money. We earn a living by creating value, trading our time or ideas, that's how we earn a living. Think of earning money as a short-term benefit for adding a long-term value to people. There is more you can give to this world than you can take from it. Ask what unique gifts and talents do you have which you could use to make the world a better place. By asking yourself this question, you are already on your way to a fulfilling and successful life.

THE POWER OF CREATIVE THINKING

Often people prefer certainty, a sense of security, a place and society where they can belong and comfortably fit in. People don't do this or that because it is risky. What if they fail at it and everyone thinks of them as a fool? So we gradually sink down to this consciousness and habit of sticking with what we know, what will not bring us failure. The C. R. A. P. principle; a situation in many people's lives that has made them victims of mediocrity and fear. Many are victims of this as opposed to being the victors. Let's start by looking at the C in the C.R.A.P.

CRITICISM: most people hate to be criticised. They hate being told it's wrong, it's not good enough and they need to try harder. Why? What do they hate about hearing all of these things? Why do they see them as blows against them as opposed to pushes towards a better self? Norman Vincent Peale had the answer when he said, "*The trouble with most of us is that we would rather be ruined by praise than saved by criticism.*"

Many people refuse to see that criticism is a positive tool that helps them sharpen their skills, their craft and perfect their work. If there were no criticism, there wouldn't be any genius in this world. That toothpick we use got tweaked many times to reach its point of sharpness; that knife you cut meat with was sharpened by the hardest knife sharpeners; and that diamond went through cutting beyond imagination.

Therefore criticism is a vital element to achieving your dreams. Like the yellow line on the road, criticism is not there to punish you but to help you drive properly to your destination with fewer or no accidents. The road to success is illuminated by the street lights of criticism, so appreciate it, learn from it, and use it as a compass to guide you on what not to do in order to become what you want to become.

Realise that whether you do good or bad, you will always have one person or more criticising you. Be receptive to criticism instead of defensive. You learn more about yourself and how to improve by taking criticism as positive feedback. What criticism means to you is entirely your choice; choose to see it as constructive feedback, view it as guidance from people around you who, aware and unaware, care for you. It is your choice to draw positive lessons from criticism and make the right changes or stick firmly to what you believe in, what liberates and resonates with your true self. Sometimes criticism is a result of people expressing their true self, which in some cases is a reflection of what the critics are suppressing in themselves. Being honest, realistic and open about your true self can make other people uncomfortable, especially those who do not believe in their dreams.

Allowing other people's opinions about you to become your reality is the worst thing you can do; it is giving someone so much power over you and your life. It is even worse when such people, the critics, are not pursuing their own dreams. Why take to heart criticism from those who have never attempted to do anything worthwhile in their lives? Bernard M. Baruch says, "Be who you are and say what you feel, because those who mind don't matter, and those who matter don't mind.

REJECTION: In any given situation, rejection is the nightmare of many people, but it is an optimist's sweet dream. Nothing has been responsible for more self-doubt, self-questioning and self-destruction than rejection. In fact, the very word 'rejection' floods the memories of many people with excruciating thoughts. Apparently these days it's easier to avoid rejection and deny yourself a learning opportunity than accept rejection and learn from it. Rejection does not define who you are, instead it helps you refine who you really are."

Just today how many rejections have you had? If rejections were marbles, how many of them do you think you have collected this year alone? Of course, no one wants to be rejected, and why? Why don't we want to be rejected? Do you see why it matters now?

People would rather be rejected in things and places society scorns. What if society rejects your true self, but not who it wants you to be? Would you still accept the rejection or be what people want you to be because you are afraid of the rejection monster?

As actress, Jennifer Aniston, said in an interview about moving into acting: "*I was told to avoid the business altogether because of the rejection. People would say to me, 'Don't you want to have a normal job and a normal family?' I guess that would be good advice for some people, but I wanted to act.*"

More often, by accepting rejection and still holding on to your goals you have rejected mediocrity. You have rejected being like everyone else; you have accepted that in life you are born to stand out instead of fitting in, and those who fit in usually reject themselves, solely because they are intimidated by people who stand out. It is not too late to start, and it's never too early to do it. You are the captain of your ship. By sitting where you are right now and not pursuing your dream, you are rejecting your true worth.

Reject rejection and turn your aspirations into reality. During the San Francisco Gold Rush in the 1840s, thousands of prospective gold miners were seeking wealth in the gold rich area. They would come from all states in search of the gold that could help them acquire the riches they wanted. Some of these miners would roam the region looking for places to mine gold. Each time they got to a place that was mined and already depleted of gold deposits, they would find a sign board written "**N**ext **O**pportunity," signaling to them that they need not waste their time shovelling there as everything had already been taken.

Some miners who got tired of leaving a lengthy message on the signpost left a signboard with "**NO**" written on it. Everyone who passed by understood the acronym. NO was later used beyond the minefields in everyday life until people forgot the origin and meaning. It was a symbol of hope for those seeking better opportunities. The signs reminded them that if they couldn't find an opportunity where they sought, they should optimistically keep searching; looking out for the *'**N**ext **O**pportunity, as it was **N**ot **O**ver yet.'* Unfortunately over the years the true meaning of this acronym was lost and it was turned into a word that symbolised a stop sign. So remember the origins of NO. Do not take NO for an answer, do not allow your dream to die inside of you, therefore, dare to dream and dare to do it.

The strategy to overcome rejection is resilience. Rather than focusing on the rejection, be objective and focus on the solutions you can create. It is not the number of punches you can take from life and society, it is the number of punches you can take, still stand up, and walk boldly and fearlessly in the direction of your destiny.

"Don't bail; the best gold is at the bottom of the barrels of crap."
Randy Bausch

ADVERSARIES: We all keep a couple of these in our lives. We don't have to invite them, they just come to the party, and they come in their varied masks. However, sometimes you can turn your adversaries into your allies. These are the people who make you question yourself; they literally make you look at yourself in the mirror and make-up your face with self-doubt.

They are treasure pirates. They are like the Forty Thieves against Ali Baba. Of course, they can always be ignored, avoided and overlooked. As you rekindle with the powerful soul within you, have a great relationship with the true you, then every adversary you encounter becomes a stepping-stone on the road that leads to the reality of your dreams. As Horace said, "*Adversity has the effect of eliciting talents, which in prosperous circumstances would have lain dormant.*"

Observe the people you spend most of your time with. Their thoughts influence the way you think and view life. If they have negative thoughts most of the time, then they are limiting your potential and reach in life. The first step to take towards your goals is to take a step away from them. Every step you take away from them is a bold step closer towards achieving your goals. When you want to soar with the eagles, you can't flock with the turkeys. Use adversity to carve yourself into an ace, as a hammer and chisel to carve you into an ace of life. Life is like a game of cards. To succeed, to be a winner, to win the gold medal, one needs to get rid of the jokers in the pack and start playing with the aces.

PRESSURE: This is a double-edged sword, because it is not how it is but how you use it. You can use it to cut through your fear to your greatness or you can use it to cut the ropes that hold the bridge to the reality of your dreams. In my opinion, there are two types of pressure, constructive pressure and destructive pressure. When you work hard towards your dream, work hard to finish your project before deadline or even work hard to beat your targets at work. That is constructive pressure. It means you are using pressure positively to fuel you towards being a better person than you already are, unleashing more potential in you.

Destructive pressure, the enemy of many people who have fallen victim to it, is when most dreams are choked or drowned. Pressure is not entirely bad. The kind of pressure we inflict on ourselves can potentially break or make us. Pressure to deliver the best project of the year so you can get your yearly bonus and take your family on holiday is a key to unlock more of your potential. It is a springboard to help you reach greater heights. When you are under pressure to reach your work targets and bag a promotion, then we say, "All the best, and give it your best shot." In this case, it is not the load that breaks you but the way you carry it.

Turn your pressure to succeed in life into your pleasure. When you put yourself under pressure because you want to achieve greater heights in life and become a respectable member of society, then you are of service to people. The only thing that pushes a bullet toward its target is the pressure of the gunpowder to propel it forward. Use your pressure to propel your courage to move you forward in life, to unlock your unlimited potential, to explore your unlimited possibilities and achieve beyond your dreams. Utilise pressure as a positive asset that helps you move mountains and soar as high as eagles. Put on yourself the pressure that propels you to charge towards your dreams and become the person you aspire to be.

The now billionaire, Jack Ma, with his adventurous spirit and witty sense of humour probably went through more C. R. A. P. than any other individual who believed in the power of a dream and how it could change the world. What was once a dream in his mind is today a mammoth global company that employs over twenty-eight thousand people in China, and turned over more than US$ 9 billion in annual sales revenue in 2014 alone.

Today, in some way or another, Jack's idea has impacted on many lives and continues to revolutionise the world of e-commerce. His idea has turned him into a billionaire, and he enjoys a seat in the Forbes billionaires club. Alibaba is now a company rubbing shoulders with the Fortune 500 mammoths. The foundations of Jack's idea are nowhere close to its success today. If anyone in modern times has endured more criticism, rejection, adversity and pressure in pursuit of a dream, it should be Jack Ma. His effort and determination to turn what he believed in into reality now overwhelms even those whose imagination could not comprehend the possibility of what is now a giant e-commerce company.

Jack's story is not glamorous. He was born in the Hangzhou, Zhejiang Province, China, and grew up as a bright and promising child, bubbling with intelligence and curiosity. The young Jack at age twelve used to spend his summer holidays as a tour guide for American tourists who came to visit Hangzhou and in exchange for his services they taught him how to speak English. It was through these tour guides that he learned much about western ways of business and thinking and it was here where he crafted fundamental principles and values that would guide his life.

From an early age Jack was an intelligent child with numerous ideas. At some point his father told him that if he had been born thirty years earlier with all his ideas, during the culture revolution era of China, he would have gone to jail. He spent much of his time studying and learning the English language. He later went to study for a bachelor's degree in English, attending the Hangzhou Teacher's Institute, where he failed three times before getting admission. He later worked as an English teacher at the Hangzhou Dianzi University.

Before getting his big break in business, Jack certainly endured a hefty blow of rejections. He was rejected by Harvard University about ten times. When KFC opened its first restaurant in Hangzhou, he was among the first twenty-four people to apply. All the other twenty-three got a job and he was rejected. He was amongst five people who applied for a job as a police officer. If also got rejected, told that he was not good enough. In his own words:

"Never give up. Today is hard, tomorrow will be worse, but the day after tomorrow will be sunshine."

While visiting the United States of America in 1995, Jack first learnt of the Internet, not knowing how to use the keyboard. His colleague asked him to type anything he wanted on the search engine. A bit nervous that he would break the computer, he was reluctant, however he gave it a try. From that day, although the Internet was not yet introduced in China, he knew it would become big business one day and he felt a conviction to start an Internet business when he went back home to China.

Starting off with only seventeen other partners, Jack was determined to make his company one of the largest e-commerce retail companies in the world. The early years are a far cry from what his company is today. Enduring more criticism than most of his counterparts, he put his head down and worked diligently. The optimistically predicted downfall of Alibaba inspired such comments as '*This is the most stupid idea you've ever had,*' which perhaps implied that Jack as an English teacher would never succeed in big business.

Much criticism, rejection, adversity and pressure from the media and competitors were endured by Jack Ma while tenaciously building his company, which he started in 1999. To the amazement of his critics, in September 2014 Alibaba became the most valuable tech company in the world, raising $25 billion from its United States Initial Public Offering (IPO) at the New York Stock Exchange. Today Jack Ma often recites his business philosophy, "*Customer number one, employee number two and shareholder number three.*" He is worth $22 billion and regularly gets lecture invitations from top universities worldwide such as Harvard University and Wharton School of Business. In the words of the movie icon, Forrest Gump, "Life is like a box of chocolates. You will never know what you're going to get."

With great a self-belief and acknowledging that failure would play a vital role in making Alibaba the 'the most customer-centric company', Jack was willing to experiment, be rejected, fail and learn from his failures as the company grew. While thinking what name to give his company, Jack concluded that he would name it *Alibaba*, after the famous fable of 'Open Sesame', because he believed the Internet was open for all. Over the years the symbolism and the might of that name has also epitomised the growth of the company. Alibaba symbolises the greatness of the vision of Jack Ma's company. It has also been a symbol of an open sesame with over 400 million small businesses registered on Alibaba.

Today Alibaba, despite many critics anticipating its downfall, has borne witness to its rapid growth to become the largest Chinese e-commerce company. From merely one guy with a dream and seventeen investors, a grand vision has turned into a grand reality. On reflecting back to the hard beginnings of his company, he is still passionate about teaching. He is adamant about using technology to empower young people in his company, and refers to himself as the (CEO) Chief Educational Officer of Alibaba.

"*Everything is possible.*"
Jack Ma

DO YOU HAVE LIMITS OR BOUNDARIES?

There are no limits in this world, there are only boundaries, and the beauty of this is that boundaries can always be transcended. People beat themselves down, burden themselves with illusions of grandeur and false notions of happiness and fulfilment without realising that all those things happen when you let go of when and how you will be happy and fulfilled and realising that you have the power to be all of those things right now.

Life is an assignment and your lifetime is the time you have to fulfill this course; your purpose. Ever seen students procrastinating with their assignments for a time they have set in future? The whole time they are idling, frustrated and trying not to think of the assignments that they have put aside, put behind or placed somewhere in the future. This is true in reality. We put our purpose aside, or behind us, with some illusion that we will commit to it in some near future without realising that happiness begins when you commit yourself to your course, your calling, your purpose in life.

To transform your life from self-limiting beliefs to positively empowering self-fulfilling prophecies is to realise that you do not have any limits, you only have boundaries. This is a first step to self-awareness and potential discovery. The only limits you have are the ones you have set for yourself in your consciousness. The great thing, on the other hand, is that they are not at all limits, they are boundaries to a greater space and place in your life that you can get to whenever you decide to transcend all your self-imposed fears.

What exactly do you fear? When you take time to ponder upon this question you will realise that all the things you think you fear do not exist, they are merely images you have created in your mind and they do not exist in reality. Fear is a signal that you are using your creative imagination negatively to create self-limiting beliefs in your life instead of using your creative imagination positively to create self-fulfilling prophecies in your life. When you focus your mind on the feelings that make you happier, healthier and excited about life, you create an experience in yourself that shifts your mind-set into the right state of the mind.

The distance between where you are right now and where you are supposed to be is not a limit; it is a boundary and a bridge of courage bridges all boundaries. When you realise that you don't have a dead-end but an end-goal, everything becomes a means to that goal.

"It is our duty as men and women to proceed as though the limits of our abilities do not exist."
Pierre Teilhard de Chardin

As you change your mind-set, you change the direction of your life and the course of your life. Limiting beliefs will positively transform into empowering self-fulfilling prophecies. It is not about the resources you have at your disposal, it is about how resourceful you can be with the resources at your disposal.

The laws of physics advocate that aerodynamically, the bumblebee shouldn't be able to fly, but the bumblebee doesn't know it, so it goes on flying anyway. Therefore, be whatever you want to be, do whatever you want to do and go wherever you want to go, because you too do not know of any limits. Be like the bumblebee. You become what you think about at all times and the greatest resource you have in this world is your thoughts. As you start realising that you are destined for greatness, your life becomes more meaningful and every experience becomes rewarding and empowering.

ALLEGORY OF THE COIN

When someone comes to me saying they have a problem, I ask them if they have a problem or is that merely how they view the situation. It *is* merely a situation after all. *How* you view it is what determines what it is. They say finding yourself between the devil and the deep blue sea, this is a golden opportunity for you to learn either how to swim or to fire walk. If I took out a coin and put it on the table and you only saw the tail side of it, does that make the whole coin a tail? No, that is only what you see at that moment. If I put a situation on the table and you only saw the problem side of it, does that make the whole situation a problem? No, that is only what you see at that moment. Moral of the story: Change your attitude towards your circumstances in life and the circumstances in your life will change. Life is always good on the flip side of things. Moral of the story; The days of the, '*survival of the fittest*' are numbered and the count down has begun. A new era is rising, and that is, '*the survival of the smartest.*' While the fittest will strive to survive, the smartest will thrive. When your thinking is right, your world will be right.

THE WILL TO WIN

Finally, when you decide you are going to do something outstanding with your life, pursue your lifelong conviction and dream, the naysayers pitch up and tell you it is impossible, it is not going to happen, it is going to be hard. They forgot to mention that it is not going to be difficult either. In fact, inch by inch, every step you take towards it is going to be worth it. The path is not meant to be easy, it is meant to be worth it. Those who give up at the first touch of hardship, those who fall at the blow of the first punch, will never taste the sweetness of victory or their destiny. Those who give up the course do so at the expense of their dream, their life fulfilment and purpose.

They are unaware that they are willing to endure a sad life of regret and the haunting curiosity of what could have been. Some say they fear failure, yet by not taking the first step towards their dream they have already failed. When you turn your fear of failure into your curiosity for failure, you give yourself the opportunity to learn from it. When you forego your dreams out of fear of failure, you will endure a painful life of regret. The pain of a lifetime of regret will always outweigh the pain of a temporary defeat. Learning to look at your failure's intrinsic value instead of its face value will help you discover the positive and valuable lessons you can harvest from your failures. These lessons can help you achieve great results, knocking down your perceptions of brick walls.

"I'm addicted to winning. The more you win, the more you want to win."
Larry Ellison

It is not how hard you fall; it is how high you are willing to rise when you finally stand up again that makes all the difference. The darkest hour of the night is the one right before dawn, the hardest punches are the ones before victory and the heaviest footsteps are the ones before the finish line. Do not give up on your goals, it is the hardships you endure along the way that increase the intrinsic value of your victory. All bitter battles end with sweeter victories. Fight until your last breathe, until your punches are heavy and the only voice cheering you on is the one deep inside of you. When the going gets tough, tougher people will get going. Hold on to your dream, the realisation of it will be the only legacy you will leave in this world, the only memory the next generations will have of you and the only deed that will ever inspire your generation.

Ignore the voices that beat you down, listen to the voices that cheer you up and give you a pat on the shoulder. They are the well from which you draw strength. You are born to do something special with your life and to leave the world a better place than you found it. You can never dream and not be blessed with the abilities to make that dream come true. Believe in yourself, believe in your dream. It is not what it takes to achieve your dream, it is what you are willing to put in, to make your dream happen. In the end, amidst all adversity, all trials and tribulations, you only look at yourself in the mirror.

Either you stand for what you truly believe in, your dream, or you fall for anything. Never allow caution to override conviction. Keep fighting for your dream. Every day is an opportunity to build your dream. Use your passion to succeed; it is easier to excel when you are passionate. Passion makes life easier and more rewarding. The simplest and fastest way to be successful is to make a living by doing what you are passionate about.

A simple recipe for success is to seek and find your passion. Turn that passion into your purpose:

PURPOSE + VISION + AMBITION + PASSION + CONVICTION = PROSPERITY

Always bear in mind and hold in your heart, that you are the candle that must illuminate this world. Don't allow anyone or anything to put out the fire in you. In the words of Ayn Rand, in her book *The Fountainhead*, 1943:

"It is not the works, but the belief which is here decisive and determines the order of rank - to employ once more a religious formula with a new and deeper meaning, - it is some certainty which a noble soul has about itself, something which is not to be sought, is not to be found and perhaps, also not to be lost - The noble soul has reverence for itself."- (Friedrich Nietzsche, Beyond Good and Evil)

"This view of man has rarely been expressed in human history. Today, it is virtually non-existent. Yet this is the view with which in various degrees of longing, wistfulness, passion and agonised confusion — the best of mankind's youth start out in life. It is not even a view, for most of them, but a foggy, groping, undefined sense made of raw pain and incommunicable happiness. It is a sense of enor-

mous expectation, the sense that one's life is important, that great achievements are within one's capacity and that great things lie ahead.

"It is not in the nature of man — nor of any living entity to start out by giving up, by spitting in one's own face and damning existence; that requires a process of corruption whose rapidity differs from man to man. Some give up at the first touch of pressure; some sell out; some run down by imperceptible degrees and lose their fire, never knowing when or how they lost it. Then all of these vanish in the vast swamp of their elders who tell them persistently that maturity consists of abandoning one's own mind; security, of abandoning one's values; practicality, of losing self-esteem. Yet a few hold on and move on, knowing that fire is not to be betrayed, learning how to give it shape, purpose and reality. But whatever their future, at the dawn of their lives, men seek a noble vision of man's nature and of life's potential.

"There are very few guideposts to find. The Fountainhead *is one of them*

"This is one of the cardinal reasons of The Fountainhead's *lasting appeal: It is a confirmation of the spirit of youth, proclaiming man's glory, showing how much is possible.*

"It does not matter that only a few in each generation will grasp and achieve the full reality of man's proper stature — and that the rest will betray it. It is those few that move the world and give life it's meaning and it is those few that I have always sought to address. The rest are no concern of mine; it is not me or The Fountainhead *that they will betray: It is their own souls."*

THE SKY IS THE BOUNDARY

"They say the sky is the limit… the actual truth is that you do not have limits, only boundaries. And the beauty of boundaries is that they can always be transcended."

Most people will extol, reasonably, why they cannot achieve their goals in life, why they have not achieved them, or why they will never achieve them. They might even write a thesis with well-researched excuses on why they cannot achieve those goals, listing the obstacles instead of levers to success. Such people have invested much of their time, effort and energy in finding all those excuses. The amazing part of their thesis is that it makes complete sense to them. The reality is that we live in a world and an era where the permission and inspiration to dream big and achieve all the goals we have set for ourselves to achieving is unlimited. You can never know what you are capable of unless you try doing something every day that you thought you were incapable of doing. It is not the sky that is the limit; it is your own imagination.

Ironically, many people have never checked the other side of the coin; they haven't spun it enough to see the other side of it. They have not done enough introspection or found all the reasons why they could achieve their goals and how in fact they are going to achieve them. They say, 'I am not ready,' 'I am not good enough,' 'I need to know more people,' 'I need to drive that car first,' 'I need to get that job first' and then they will be ready to achieve their dreams.

The often great thing is that they have made peace with that way of thinking, and with the illusion that they will not achieve the goals they have set for themselves. They live everyday lives with the consciousness that they can only achieve so much. They set the bar low enough to avoid disappointment.

By setting higher goals for ourselves, higher standards for what achievement means to us, we give ourselves the inspiration to achieve beyond what we thought we could achieve, because achievement is a measure of our capabilities. The higher you set your goals, the more you are inclined to achieve them. Set higher goals for yourself, set higher standards for yourself, set higher expectations for yourself than people have set for you, because when you set the bar too high for yourself, you will be motivated and single-mindedly focused on achieving those goals. Higher standards keep you excited and hopeful to want to do more and achieve more.

The saying; the sky is the limit, is limiting by its very nature. It implies that there are no limits, yet it imposes that the sky itself is the limit. Contrary to conventional wisdom, the amazing discovery is realising that limits are self-imposed. You can achieve whatever you want to achieve, provided you channel all your energy, effort, time, intellect and passion to achieving it. When your dreams and ambitions become your purpose for living, you are bound to become successful and achieve your dream. The greatness in you can only be measured by the actions you take and the positive impact you persist to make in this world.

Perhaps the first time humankind realised that the sky was the limit, was in 1903 when the Wrights Brothers designed and flew their first successful airplane. Then it was a fact. Half a century later, in 1969, was to be the last time the sky would ever be the limit, when Neil Armstrong and Buzz Aldrin pierced right through the sky to land on the moon. Since then, the sky has been the boundary, a gateway to more that is yet to be explored and discovered. Fast-forward another half a century, mankind is heading for Mars. Although progress has proven to be a slow process.

These series of events in history; giant leaps in the last century, the feverishly inventive imagination and the insatiable curious nature of human beings is proving over and over again that we do not have limits. Therefore, the sky is not the limit — the only limits you have, the only limits you have ever had and the only limits you will ever have are the ones you impose on yourself. No one told you that you cannot achieve the goals you have set for yourself. Even if someone has, it's your choice to take their flimsy opinion and make it your reality. You have a choice, and whichever one you choose, it is right. Your success is determined by you and only you.

Sometimes you ought to wonder whether you see afar because you are standing on a giant's shoulders, or is it because you are a giant yourself? Envision and embrace yourself as the latter. The conformists of this world preach that you should know your limits and work within them. However, the most concerning thought has been, how can people really know their limits unless they try to expand them and push some boundaries?

A lot of people today who have not achieved their dreams, resort to being successful negative storytellers. They turn their failure to pursue their dreams into wonderful tales of why they did not or could not achieve their dreams. They become successful storytellers of tales of failure. They suffer from what I call Exquisites (do not worry about the dictionary now, you might never find it), a common disease among so-called losers who failed to achieve their dreams. These 'victims' have an agitating need to constantly pepper their conversations with phrases like, "It's impossible" and "The reality is" or "Be realistic about things... it won't happen." The symptoms of Exquisites are pessimism, negativity, lack of self-confidence, depression, stress and the ongoing need to bring others down.

Appreciate that the people around you are there for a reason, for a purpose. It might take a season or longer; they have a great reason why they are there at that moment and time in your life. The disease of Exquisites has held back as many people in the world as has fear. Perhaps you may know a couple of people around you who need help. Such people will make excuses instead of creating ways to achieve their goals.

The truth about all of this is that everyone knows the cure for their own Exquisites. They hold it in their hands, they have it in their heart and they know. However, they prefer to wake up every day and take a dose or two of excuses before they start their day. An apple a day keeps the doctor away, and a spoonful of excuses keeps the failures close. People need to stop giving excuses and act. Taking action is the only solution. If people act towards reaching their goals, acting towards achieving their dreams, instead of giving excuses why they are not acting, they will realise that action brings one a step closer to their dreams ambitions and aspirations. It's even easier to take action than to make excuses.

It is undoubtedly absurd that many people are more afraid of standing up and achieving their goals than sitting down and doing nothing. They want to 'play it safe'. The truth however, is that in pursuit of your dreams, aspirations and ambitions, the most dangerous way to play it, is to play it safe. It is mind crippling, physically disabling and spiritually and morally destructive. Playing it safe is the most dangerous way to play it. The only security in life is at the heart of risk, risking is the safest way to play. The only place that is safe in life is life after death.

An inspirational entrepreneur is the first South African to be awarded the World Entrepreneur of the Year for Managing Change by Ernest and Young. He is a serial entrepreneur, seasoned dealmaker, a businessman and the first ever black South African to own and run a foreign exchange company in South Africa. His company captured about 10% of the country's market and grossed annual revenue in excess of $212 million. K. K. Combi's start is a far cry from the accolades and achievements he possesses today.

Born in a small township in Tokai in Cape Town at the height of apartheid, his family was forcibly moved to the township of Gugulethu when he was merely six years old, an event, which he admits today, left an emotional scar. Reminiscing on that event, he shares his deepest feelings: "My family, like many others at the time, was a victim of forced removals. It was one of the most traumatic events of my life, and today still leaves me feeling angry, particularly because of the level of brutality that was involved."

He still vividly remembers how the then police force would stop by every house and tell everyone to take their personal possessions and move. At that early age, he was not only a victim but a witness of how his family went from having a decent house to a small shack and being thrown into the poverty-stricken township of Gugulethu. Unlike most people who bore witness to this event, K. K. decided not to stay at the bottom of the food chain. He realised early that if he did not live the life he desired, he only had himself to blame. Instead of this crippling his spirit, it fuelled his desire to change his circumstances. In the middle of this sad situation, K. K. landed his first job as an insurance salesman for one of the country's biggest insurance companies. With an entrepreneurial zeal and an eye for lucrative opportunities, K. K. carved his own niche market in the insurance space and profited handsomely. Realising that he could sell insurance only to black people at that time due to the state of the country, he concluded that the only people that could help him achieve his sales quota were teachers, nurses and policemen, since they were the only black people who had stable employment.

K.K.'s burning enthusiasm to succeed and rise to the top earned him Best Salesman of the Year, and a great commission for his outstanding enterprises. Having slogged his guts out as an insurance salesman and accumulating sizeable capital, eighteen months later K. K. left his job as an insurance salesman to start a self-service café in the township of Gugulethu. The business operated well for a while. However, it was short-lived due to the political unrest. Left with little choice, he sold the business and ventured into a new business. He opened the first service station in Gugulethu, which was later sold to a major oil company, and pursued other business aspirations.

"Look out for opportunities. They are always there waiting to be discovered."
Zitulele 'K. K. ' Combi

Spotting an opportunity in property, K. K. then moved into the real estate business. He is a relentless and enthusiastic entrepreneur, always looking for the next opportunity. Realising that by not being in property, he would be in poverty, a history he did not want repeated in his life, K. K. started amassing land with the idea of developing a shopping complex in his neighbourhood, which was later rejected by residents of the area. Using this stumbling block of rejection as a stepping-stone, he then rezoned the land and sold it for nine times its initial purchase price, an incident that the Tote in the horse racing arena would coin as a Golden Jackpot. After hitting this opportunity's bull's eye, he identified a station in the heart of the Cape Flats, which appealed to his property senses as a potential site to develop a shopping centre. He acquired that land and built what is now famously known as Nyanga Junction, which he later sold to another property company for dazzling millions.

With his adventures surpassing those of Tom Sawyer and with enough capital to leap into the sky, K. K. then built a bigger service station in a town deeper in the Eastern Cape of South Africa. After his hard work and deeds of bravery, K. K. decided to reward himself with a holiday to the UK where he was on a quest for new ideas. It was here in the heart of London where he found the golden goose awaiting him. While on his well-deserved vacation he discovered that due to democracy's arrival in 1994, a number of people were now travelling to South Africa. The knowledge quickly clicked as he was exchanging currency that tourists visiting South Africa, would require the service of an exchange bureau; again, he had struck the golden rock.

Coming back home and having learned the business of exchange bureau, he was compelled to venture into this business, where dollars, euros and pounds were a staple of conversation. He arranged meetings with the big guys at the Reserve Bank, who granted him a foreign exchange licence. This opened doors for him as the first black-owned foreign exchange company in South Africa. Today K. K. is a corporate captain, sitting on the boards of various listed companies. He is a board member of the country's Stock Exchange as well.

ALLEGORY OF THE GARDEN

According to conventional wisdom, '*Money does not grow on trees*'. Thus, the allegory of the garden argues that, '*Whoever said money does not grow on trees must have really been in the wrong garden*'. Money is a token of value, a means, a psychological mechanism for organising resources to realise your vision. Two American shoe salesmen, their sales manager had sent them into the Amazon rainforests to try and find a new and untapped market for their shoe brand.

On arriving in the first village, they realised that none of the natives in that village wore shoes and had no clue what shoes were. The other salesman, quick to fall victim to pessimism told his colleague, "It is very clear that we'll not make even one pair of shoes sales here. Maybe this is a sign, a blessing in disguise. We can't cast our nets in a desert oasis. We should pack our bags and head back home." The other salesman saw a different situation, an opportunity. He wondered how much sales they could make if they could employ their persuasive passion to convince the chief and the villagers to own at least a pair of their shoes. He quipped into his colleague's ear, "*Sometimes you have to walk a mile in your customer's shoes in order to feel the pain of the pebble in their shoes. In this case the pain is obvious. We are really in the right garden here, my pal. This is not a blessing in disguise, this is a blessing on the spotlight. Just put off your sunglasses and look at all this gold mine we have found ourselves in. There are more than enough feet for our shoes to fit here. More than enough fish in the sea for our nets to catch. The world is our oyster and I just so happen to love seafood.*"

In this allegory, the money is not that paper in your pocket or figures in your bank that is merely a symbolic reference of success; money is mind-set, it's the quality of your thoughts. The progressive realisation of a worthy goal, for its worthy rewards. The garden is equally a metaphor for the right state of self-belief. Often referred to as the prosperity consciousness. When a person has tuned their state of mind into a prosperity consciousness, they adopt a positive attitude that allows them to identify opportunities and strategies to seize them, which yields great achievements in their lives. Moral of the story: In any even given situation, the most optimistic, opportunistic and open-minded person will always recognise an opportunity and identify a solution to seize the opportunity.

The tree is a metaphor for the state of mind. Only a tree that is well nourished with the nutrients of a fertile soil bears good fruit. Any mind that is exposed only to positive messages is able to cultivate healthy thoughts that can be translated into desired outcomes for people's lives. A tree that grows on the edge of a cliff cannot bear good fruits. A mind that is constantly receiving negative messages cannot bear good thoughts. The mind is a wellspring of all good things to be achieved, all great dreams to be realised, so it is important that the mind be nurtured with positive messages at all times.

When the mind is focused on a definite goal in life and you give all your heart, energy and everything within you to achieving it, the achievement of such goal will in return give you everything you aspire for in the world. Just as the tree knows that the soil has in it all the nutrients to make it bear good fruits, you have all the resources you need within you to make all your dreams come true. When a seed is ready, it sprouts; when an apple is ripe, it falls from the tree. When a dream is ready, it will become a reality. As long as you do your part. When you aspire for great achievements in life, the universe will conspire in assisting and guiding you in achieving them.

The yearning within the human spirit to pursue something meaningful and more rewarding usually springs from somewhere deep within ourselves. It is a yearning for a sense of purpose. The realisation of that yearning into reality is naturally progressive; like the blossoming of a sunflower. Success is therefore the harvest of your thinking and you will reap what you have sown. As the old adage says, "*Energy flows to where the focus goes.*"

STRIKE THE IRON UNTIL IT'S HOT

"What is opportunity, and when does it knock? It never knocks. You can wait a whole lifetime, listening, hoping, and you will hear no knocking. None at all. You are your opportunity, and you must knock on the door leading to your destiny. You prepare yourself to recognise opportunity, to pursue and seize opportunity as you develop the strength of your personality, and build a self-image with which you are able to live with your self-respect alive and growing."

Dr. Maxwell Maltz

The conventional wisdom is that you should strike while the iron is still hot. Most people sit down patiently waiting for opportunities to knock at their door or perhaps be delivered to them on a silver platter. People like to follow trends, they follow the status quo and love to do what everyone is doing. If everyone is waiting with anticipation that one day the iron will get hot and they will strike it, this is quite suicidal. What if the iron never gets hot and the years go by? And by age eighty you can no longer raise the hammer with much strength by the time an opportunity finally avails itself.

It's advisable to go out there rather than wait for opportunities. Go out there, seek them, find them, and seize them! The most astonishing nature common to all opportunities is that they multiply with seizure — the more opportunities you look for and make the best of, the more opportunities avail themselves to you. The problem is that many people hesitate to do attempt great endeavours, they want things to happen to them.

Opportunities are like fragile butterflies, they only come to people who love them and bring out the best in them. They love people who are adventurous and courageous. There is nothing worth achieving in comfort zones. Opportunities are like shooting stars, always be on the look out for them. They are butterflies, also vulnerable, therefore when you have them, appreciate them. Opportunities are the vehicle for success — you attract them by being a person who is always on the hunt for them.

Envision an opportunity as an iron bar that has one half in a furnace and the other outside of it. Anyone in charge can light the furnace or switch it off, and you never know when are they going to switch the furnace off or on. You might strike and the iron is cold. Why trust that opportunities will be thrown at you? What if it never happens that way? What if you just get on with the task and start striking the iron bar? You might as well strike it instead of waiting for an opportunity. Rather do what you know to do — strike the iron until its hot!

Having practised, flexed your muscles, when that opportunity avails itself you are more than ready. So forget about striking while the iron is still hot — it might turn out that it was not meant to get hot for you. Stand up and strike that iron until it is hot. To achieve a goal, don't wait for it. When you are hungry for success in life, go out and get it because you have the strength and ability to get whatever you set your mind on and heart to.

The only thing that life, and nature, never stand in front of is perseverance — when you want to achieve a goal, have that life, or you want that job. Even in the midst of difficulties, keep chasing your goals. Even when those around you tell you, 'Mate, just give up and find something different to do.' Listen to your inner voice; keep on fighting, because only you have the power and the ability to bring your dreams into reality.

Many successful people today persevered in pursuit of their goals. They encountered great difficulties along the way; however they kept on going. People say it's not the height of the mountain that stops you from reaching the top, it is the pebble in your shoe, if only you allow it to stop you. Often people who gave up along the way say, 'No, that dude got lucky, he just had all the cards to his advantage'. Guess what? That dude had no cards, all he had were his situations and he made the best out of them.

Raymond Kroc once said, "Success is a dividend of sweat. The harder you sweat the luckier you get." Even at work, who gets the promotion? Not the lottery winner, unless it's by default, or somewhere in the universe a shooting star hits a meteorite, which is like when? Never! A German proverb says:

> "*Luck sometimes visits a fool, but it never sits down with him.*"

Some mistakes just never happen. The individual that goes that extra mile, that's the soul that is luckier. That person that puts in extra effort, does an extra job, puts in more hours, gets there earlier, leaves later and works harder than everyone else, that's the individual who gets lucky. Luck happens when life hears the loud echoes of your ambition, hard work, courage, persistence and determination and decides to meet you half way.

By working harder, doing more, putting more effort into what you do every day, you give every ounce of yourself to your work and luck will follow you wherever you are. You will soon be amazed by how much you have achieved beyond the boundaries you set for yourself.

In pursuit on your goals, the most dangerous way to play it is to play it safe. The biggest risk that people take in life is the risk of not taking risks. If we want to succeed and achieve the goals we have set for ourselves, then we must accept that disappointment, mistakes, failures and other unforeseen challenges are part of the journey. The road to success or personal achievement is paved with the gravel of failures, mistakes and disappointments. However, our willingness to persist to move forward, to persevere, sets us apart from the ordinary individuals who have settled for what life throws at them.

Those multitudes of individuals who lack perseverance and persistence, especially when the odds seem to be against them, end up settling for mediocrity. They give up, even though they have only tried once or twice. They fail to acknowledge that it is as much effort to lose as it is to win. They lose the race not because they started late but because they lacked the personal drive to reach the finish line. As Elias Ballard notes in her story about Esther Pearl:

"You have a mission. The mission is renewal. You are proof that death and dehumanisation didn't prevail, that there is life after an atrocity and that there must be joy in life that is lived after atrocity. It's not just about surviving; it's about reviving. It's a spark, of bringing an essence of vitality into the world...Because you better do big things, nothing in life could just be good enough, because if you were just good enough, you didn't survive. Only if you were really big, really daring, really cunning, really determined — and lucky — would you survive. Halfway didn't get you there."

People never fail in life or never reach their goals in life because they are born losers. People do not become losers the moment they fail, they are losers the moment they give up on chasing their dreams. The word *'impossible'* only exists in the dictionary and minds of losers. If there is one thing that history and all its victors have taught us it is that everything is possible; with enough courage and perseverance nature is bound to make way for those few rare souls who push past it with great might.

To succeed in achieving your aspirations, you ought to conquer what conventional wisdom and its naïve followers have written in the history books as *impossible*, always going beyond the extra mile in order to prove them otherwise. Although many people never persevere long enough or hard enough, they should learn from those who have gone beyond the extra mile. In all the miles one ought to take to reach one's aspirations, it's only beyond the extra mile success begins. It is the only place where the greener pastures have not been grazed, the only territory where only the successful rest, being non-conformists, embracing endurance, persistence, and going beyond the extra mile to achieve their ambitions. Victory and success in this world belong to the most persistent individuals.

"You will never do anything in this world without courage.
It is the greatest quality of the mind next to honour."
James Allen

Among many an individual that has broken not only all the chains of societal stereotypes and conventional wisdom as well should be John Paul Dejoria. He tenaciously worked himself out of the rat hole, from being a homeless man with a child to becoming one of America's most admired billionaires. How did he go from homeless to billionaire?

John Paul's story sounds like an excerpt from one of Horatio Alger's masterpieces. At the tender age of twenty-three, the time when many young adults are trying to graduate from college, John was a perfect fit for the conventional stereotype of someone who only had a high school diploma and nothing more apart from his poverty tag, barely making a living, earning a salary insufficient to take care of his wife and child and himself. His wife left him along with his two and half year old son while at the same time he was being evicted for not paying the rent for his apartment. After being evicted, the struggling man moved into a borrowed car with his son. He scraped through by collecting soda pop bottles and selling them to a recycling company for five cents apiece just to get a meal for the day.

Although his was in the gloom of poverty, John Paul was not going to give up or allow his son to starve. He realised that he had to take responsibility for his life and that of his son and to make sure that his son had a better life and upbringing than he had. In one of his interviews he said, "We were down and out, I had a child to feed... there was no time for poor me."

Pulling himself together and evaluating his strengths and how he could profit from them, John Paul realised that his hard-working character and street smartness were the power tools that he could use to pull himself out of poverty. A son of immigrant parents who divorced when he was only two years old, raised by his mother in Echo Park, east of Los Angeles, he had been sent to a foster home because his mother was unable to care for him. As if these hard knocks were not enough, his academic life did not enjoy much applause either. While in school writing an exam, his teacher caught him red-handed passing notes to his classmate, not the best thing to be caught doing, especially when he had a sour relationship with his teachers. Having caught John Paul in this misdemeanour, his teacher ridiculed them in front of the whole class. "These two students will never, ever succeed at anything in life."

At the age of nine years, John crafted in himself the art and skill of survival; he sold Christmas cards, newspapers, photo-copy machines, encyclopedias, medical equipment, everything that he could sell, even insurance, to get his next meal. His background was not going to stop him from making a decent life for himself. His fundamental principle about success and rejection is encapsulated in his statement: "*You knock on a door fifty times, they slam it in your face. Be as enthusiastic on the fifty-first door as you were on the first door. Successful people do all the things that unsuccessful people are not willing to do, like staying enthusiastic when you are getting rejected.*"

Later on as a single and homeless parent with a son looking up to him, John gathered his hardworking ethic, creativity and business acumen to fuel himself forward into a better life. In his story, he explains that he would juggle between jobs during his early days trying to make ends meet. "I did everything from selling insurance, and I worked for Connecticut General and Hancock at the same time. I drove a linen truck around. I worked for Dictaphone! I worked for A. B. Dick, which was a photocopy company. I ended up working for Time as a circulation manager at age twenty-six."

Although life was getting better and John was starting to make a decent living, he realised that he wasn't going to wait for a golden opportunity in order to turn his life around, he had to go out there and create a golden opportunity for himself. Simply put, he went out to strike the iron until it was hot. With a growing hunger and drive to succeed, John curiously approached his then manager. "I asked my boss what it takes to be a vice-president and he said, 'Well, you are twenty-six years old, you are a high school graduate, but no college. Come back and ask me in ten years when you are around thirty-five.'" John concluded that this was certainly not a life he wanted to live and he didn't want to work for that company as far as into his thirties.

The beginnings of a new life kicked in when one of his friends helped him find a job as a salesman for a hair care products company, which was a great opportunity for him. He concluded that it was in his job that he would learn skills that would later help him to be in a position to run his own company. A couple of years later as a hair products salesman, John and his hairdresser friend, Paul Mitchell, joined forces to start a hair products company. Jointly contributing capital into their business with the last of their hard earned last savings, Paul Mitchell contributed $350 of the capital and John Paul brought in his $350. The now successful John Paul Mitchell Systems hair care products opened up shop selling its products in the hair care industry.

With complete control over his life and destiny, John Paul realised that the only way to never repeat history was to work harder and serve his customer a better product. He wanted his customers not to buy his product once; he wanted them to buy as many times as possible because he was not in the selling business, he was in the reselling business. As he says, "*You don't want to be in the order business. You want to be in the reorder business. Big difference. My goal was not to sell something to somebody. My goal was to sell something that was so good that they would want to order it again. And that's the idea that we came up with.*"

The first two years of business were quite hard he admits. No one wanted to invest in their business and they did not have enough money to pay for high-end branding and the marketing of their products. With little budget in hand, they designed their hair care bottles in the company's now iconic black and white, for the business reason that it was more affordable for them to print black and white than use colour. The other materials, which they used to make their hair care products, were bought from their suppliers on thirty-day terms, which gave them time to make some money to pay their creditors. Under pressure to turn their company into a success, John Paul employed the sales skills he had crafted and cultivated while working for his previous employer, this time with more passion and determination to turn his life around forever. He went knocking on doors, selling door to door their hair care products. Paul Mitchell also went to the salons he knew to persuade them to sell and distribute their products.

By not working hard to realise your dreams, you might be unawarely working hard to realise your own nightmares.

Eventually after more than one many knocked-on doors, innumerable rejections and uncompromising resilience, their company started growing impressively. It took them two years to pay their creditors on time and have an extra two thousand in the business account to wipe off their hard-work sweat. Gradually their company grew until they made a billion dollars in annual turnover and their products were being sold in over one hundred thousand salons in more than a hundred countries worldwide. Today John Paul Mitchell Systems is a household brand in the hair care industry and employs thousands of people globally. In 2004, John Paul Dejoria was inducted into the Horatio Alger

Association of Distinguished Americans as a lifetime member for his inspirational "rages to riches" success story and became the first individual in the professional beauty industry to receive this prestigious honour.

Like any billionaire who has acquired a taste for the finer things in life, John Paul lives now with his family in his villa in Texas. He has diversified his investments into various businesses, most famously the Patron, currently the world's number one selling brand of premium tequila, a stake in African and Thailand oil through his holding company, Madagascar Oil. He defies the conventional wisdom; 'S*trike while the iron is still hot.*' If John Paul had waited for the right opportunity, the right time and, perhaps, the excuse of many people, the right age or even weather, he would most definitely still be waiting for the Success bus to arrive.

John Paul had a sense of urgency in his life. He knew to be successful that he had to do today what other people would much rather do tomorrow, and do immediately what other people were not prepared to do. He never waited for an opportunity to make itself available for him to seize it. Unlike most people, he created his own opportunity in life and gave it his best shot. Today he lives his life on his own terms; he is master of his own destiny. In one interview he advised that people should believe in themselves and what they do and accept rejection as part of success. Anyone who wants to succeed in life must understand that they are going to have to deal with a lot of rejection as part of their day-to-day life. In addition they should cultivate a burning enthusiasm to keep going forward with resilience and determination to succeed in spite of all odds.

Sometimes the best person you can be in your life is Nobody. Because it means you have an opportunity to be a Somebody. Whether you stay a Nobody or become a Somebody, the ball is in your court. So do not use hours to make up for enthusiasm, instead use enthusiasm to make up for the hours. Many people who strongly believe in their goals, against all odds will find a way of making them come true.

"When you start with next to nothing, all you've got is a lot of thought, a lot of innovation, figuring new ways to do things without using a lot of money."
John Paul Dejoria

EDUCATION AND INFORMATION

"There is no wealth more rewarding than education and information. Seek it, find it, it will enlighten and liberate you forever!"

The word '*education*' is derived from the Latin word '*educo*' or '*educere*' which is derived from two roots, '*e*' which means 'out of' and '*ducere*' meaning to 'draw out from within' or to 'lead forth'. This presupposes that each of us from birth, in our own unique and special way is already naturally intelligent, talented and gifted. And through the process of education we are guided on how to bring it out, translate and transform this intelligence into something that is meaningful and worth value. Education is therefore a pruning tool for the tree of the mind so that it can bear good fruits. In the words of Albert Einstein, "Everybody is a genius. But if you judge a fish by its ability to climb a tree, it will live its whole life believing that it is stupid."

Benjamin Franklin once said, "*Investment into knowledge is the only investment that yields the highest return.*" And Jim Rohn, one of the most honoured authors and motivational speakers, complemented those words when he said, "*Formal education will earn you a living and self-education will earn you a fortune.*" I firmly hope these two bits of wise advice have been engraved deep in your mind and heart.

Many curious people know that as they graduate a door opens for more knowledge, more opportunities to learn about things and read books so as to develop an awareness that is wider. Avoiding a life of tunnel vision curved by conventional education is imperative. That must be replaced by an infinite striving for personal development in which you can absorb books on such development in order to further widen your knowledge base, awareness and consciousness of abundance, health and wealth, of success, of everything in the world that piques your curiosity.

Although people might invest their time and money in entertainment, I still firmly hold that the best entertainment to invest in is knowledge and personal development. Individuals who know are more aware of things, more competitive and, most importantly, more aware of opportunities around them. Their wealth of knowledge rewards them with even better knowledge of the world around them, the abundant opportunities that exist and how to seize such opportunities. Knowledge in itself is not power, it is what you do with the knowledge that is power, for action sets the energy of knowledge into motion.

So although most people have a not so positive attitude towards education and knowledge, I firmly believe that an attitude towards knowledge is a reflection of an attitude towards success. The amount of knowledge you possess about the field you want to be successful in will determine the amount of success you can achieve.

Hence it is an incontestable notion that there is no wealth as rewarding as education and information; therefore seek it, find it, and it will, undoubtedly, enlighten and liberate you forever. Have you ever wondered why the many successful in the world have libraries in their homes, and why reading these books is second nature to them? They know that it is in books where one finds the true secrets to unlocking potential and it is in those books where the true principles of rare and yet valuable knowledge is found; libraries are the true treasure islands.

The most valuable asset that one can claim ownership of in this world is yourself. Therefore the greatest investment should be in developing and growing yourself through self-education, so that you can continually grow to become a valuable citizen and a role model. Although one of the biggest prohibiters to realising our full potential and exploring the dynamism of our intelligence is lack of knowledge, the onus is within ourselves to continue taking an interest in the knowledge of things far and beyond the boundaries of what we have been taught and learned.

One of the primary reasons that we use a minimal portion of our possible intellectual potential is primarily due to the sad structure of our education system, which places so much emphasis on external testing, standardised achievement, benchmarking of intelligence, and continually forcing children to dedicate their intellectual capacities to achieving other people's goals.

Education is critical in shaping and preparing the mindset to create a better reality for itself and using such learning to create a life that one desires. Our current education system does, in fact, defeat the purpose of fundamental education. When education teaches you to accept things as they are as opposed to questioning them, going into them, giving your mind and your heart into finding other ways of thinking, then it limits imagination, shrinks intellectual capacity and narrows logical thinking, prerequisite ingredients for success.

Our thirst for knowledge should be unquenchable. The purpose of education should be to liberate, to ignite the spark of the spirit of curiosity as opposed to killing it; it should captivate imagination by embracing creativity. When education teaches us to look beyond the naked eye, to question everything, and use our cognitive abilities to continually seek new meanings of what we see, feel and touch, then education is moving you forward. Unfortunately classroom education is not designed to create thinkers; it is a factory process designed to create people that can be productive and efficient in upholding the economic status quo. Our modern day academic institutions are completely different from those of the days of Plato and Socrates, which encouraged and emphasised true education as an environment that forms the foundation and playground to fuel independent and creative thinking.

What modern day education has become is a benchmarking, process driven, labelling and standardisation process. Imagine a manufacturing plant that produces standardised goods on a massive scale and packages them, taking them through quality and standard checks to ascertain that the product is ready and fit for corporate consumption. This, of course, is an efficient model for an industrial economy; above all, a homicidal model for the true values and bases of education and intelligence.

Education beyond conventional school is what one must embrace; college degrees and qualifications are indeed a basis of education and developing the mind and certain skills for survival. However, the discipline of seeking knowledge beyond the prescribed academic curricula is what separates successful people from under-achievers. One reason many people never get far in life is because of their holding on to the old adage '*ignorance is bliss*'. Unfortunately in this day and age, where information is readily available, ignorance is culpable suicide. It is the foundation of poverty, and intellectual poverty is a plague that can lead an individual into self-destructing turmoil.

The truth we must face is that with so much information readily available from different media and with technology making information easily accessible, we are at the disposal of what we can simply call divine power. *Knowledge in itself is not power, power is what you do with the knowledge*. Knowledge is portable wealth, it is something that no one can take away from you; ironically, even if the learners defaulted on their student loans, the banks, unfortunately, would not be able to repossess their knowledge and sell it at auction. Knowledge is the only tool that gives every human being the ability to use the most powerful tool known to human beings, the brain.

Success by its simplest definition is a state of mind; human beings who seek to be a success in society starts first by empowering themselves. They understand that their professional success is entirely dependent upon their personal development. This means understanding that education is the only tool that can shape, sharpen and harness the mind to achieve whatever goals are being set. A chief culture in prominent households is to have a library. Why is this? This is because successful people understand that education does not start and end at academic institutions. Rather education is an ongoing part of life. The brain is a muscle that must constantly be exercised and flexed to keep it strong and healthy.

A university graduate, upon his graduation day, proudly leaned to whisper in his friend's ear. "This is the last time I will ever have to deal with books in life. I am done. Catch me opening a book, give me a rope, I will do the honours." This is the attitude prevalent among many people upon their graduation; their perception is that education, or rather books, are some form of punishment that imprisons them and stops them from enjoying their well-deserved youth.

Knowledge in its nature is truly a powerful force; it is the only seed that can grow a forest of bamboo trees out of a desert. Therefore, understanding that it is the best investment we can make into the future of our country, its well-being and wealth, is important. Making an investment in education empowers and enlightens us. The discipline of making the right sacrifices today in order to live the life we desire tomorrow should be a habit that spreads throughout our country, in our families and communities. The beauty of our future is entirely dependent upon the investment we are willing to make in ourselves to become valuable resources in society.

Born in the small town of Dunfermline in Scotland, and later migrating to the United States with his parents in search of a better life, or in his case the American Dream, Andrew Carnegie is renowned as an industrialist, businessman and philanthropist who is widely credited by Napoleon Hill as someone who brought to his attention *'The New Thought'*. What is even more remarkable about Andrew Carnegie are the values that were enshrined in him from as early as the age of eleven. Perhaps if it were not for a Colonel James Anderson's generosity we wouldn't know today one of the wealthiest persons in history. Colonel

Anderson believed that all those who acquire the ability to take full possession of their own minds may take possession of anything else to which they are justly entitled.

While working as a messenger in Pittsburgh, Andrew Carnegie had long since cultivated in himself the value of self-development through reading books, although he used to work until very late and never earned enough of a salary to enjoy buying books that could enrich his life. Nevertheless Andrew knew the value of education and the possibilities and opportunities it could open for him. However, like a miracle, he met Colonel James Anderson who opened up for him the treasures of literature that would unfold his intelligence, imagination and, most importantly, his true potential.

The colonel, who had more than four hundred volumes, promised he would open his library to young boys so they could read on Saturdays when they were not working. Although Andrew heard from his friend, Thomas Miller, that the colonel had opened his library for the 'working boys', he was eager to know if even he who did not work with his hands would be allowed access to this divine power. To his amazement Andrew learned that boys of his calibre too would be given access to the library, which gave him a sense of excitement and hope for growth and development in his life.

Through the permission of Colonel Anderson, Andrew knew 'the windows were opened in the walls of his dungeon through which the light of knowledge could stream in' and from then on his late nights at work a book kept him company. Every day he felt renewed and optimistic in reading a book, knowing that the next Saturday, upon completion of one volume, he could borrow another book to continue his exciting journey of enlightenment. Books to Andrew served as a torch that lit brightly into his future and were a guiding compass to his true greatness.

Later on in his life, after amassing great wealth and becoming the second wealthiest person in the world of his time, Andrew Carnegie, in honour of and gratitude to the person that taught him the value of good education through continually reading and empowering himself to become a person in society, built a monument to Colonel James Anderson to thank him for his generosity. Today that monument stands in front of the hall and library in Diamond Square and is inscribed:

"To Colonel James Anderson, Founder of Free Libraries in Western Pennsylvania. He opened his library to working boys and upon Saturday afternoons acted as librarian, thus dedicating not only his books but also himself to the noble work. This monument is erected in grateful remembrance by Andrew Carnegie, one of the "working boys" to whom were thus opened the precious treasures of knowledge and imagination through which youth may ascend."

Andrew Carnegie had what the Greeks call a sense of *philosophia*, the love of knowledge. He spent his leisure time reading books in order to educate himself beyond formal education, understanding the power of knowledge and how it can change society for the better. Upon his retirement, he geared most of his philanthropic courses to education and social development initiatives. To further extend his gratitude to Colonel Anderson and his appreciation of education, after Andrew Carnegie sold his company, Carnegie Steel, for $480 million in 1901, he dedicated the remainder of his years to donating all his money to improving society. He began by building what is now the Carnegie Mellon University in Pittsburgh, Pennsylvania, which enrols more than thirteen thousand students in different academic disciplines. What Andrew Carnegie bequeathed is a gift that keeps on giving; through education more people have become empowered and led successful lives in their respective fields, creating a society of able men and women who can think independently and contribute positively to society.

"As the twig is bent the tree's inclined."

Growing in a family of modest means with a mill-worker father and a, mother who made a living by mending shoes, Andrew saw the possibilities that education could open for him. Although he never had a formal education or graduated with a degree, his efforts, his generosity and belief in the power of education to change the world has led to more than 95,000 students getting a decent education.

The possibilities that Andrew Carnegie opened through the university he built have made such an impact on global society that one can only be inspired by the passion he had to empower society, not by giving people fish but by teaching them how to fish. Through Carnegie Mellon University, the Lauder College, which he built in honour of his uncle, he remembers the one person who encouraged him to get an education and advance himself through acquiring knowledge. He further contributed copious amounts of money to build libraries across the country and in his native country Scotland where he also shared with future generations what Colonel Anderson shared with him when he was young, the gift of knowledge.

Engraved at Carnegie Mellon University are Andrew Carnegie's words and motto, which define the institution's accomplishments over the past century, "*My Heart is in the Work*". The university has gone on to collect honours globally, ranking as the 22nd best university in the world and the 15th best university in the United States. Its students are guests at the World Economic Forum where they share with global leaders advancements in research on science and technology. Most importantly, over the past fifteen years the university's faculty, students and alumni have been credited with creating more than 300 companies and more than 9000 jobs in the country.

G*ood leaders are good readers.* Andrew Carnegie is one among many global leaders and role models who teach us the value of education and how to use it to empower ourselves to transcend beyond boundaries.

"Education is the kindling of a flame, not the filling of a vessel."
Socrates

Through a passion for education, understanding the power of knowledge and how it can be used to carve a brighter future for society, Andrew went on to dedicate his life to the this noble cause of empowering the world. His contribution, presence and vision for society still illuminates brightly through the legacy he has left for the current and future generations.

The significance of education to shape us into better individuals, respected in society, is an indispensable part of our lives, professionally, socially and personally. The need for ongoing self-education beyond formal education is what advances any individual to even greater heights. All who have risen above the common levels of society have received two kinds of education: the first from their schoolteachers, the second, more personally and importantly, from themselves by their own accord. The significance of education has been preached for millennia now, from as early as the schools of the great philosophers and the industrial revolution education to the modern day form of education where information has become a readily available resource that whoever seeks to learn can now easily accomplish with the click of a button.

In his book, *Education and Significance of Life*, Jiddu Krishnarmuti proposes an educational system, that instead of being another brick in the wall, has a well rounded approach, reflective of the true ideals of human potential; by igniting a healthy curiosity and therefore drawing out of our true intelligence:

> *"Conventional education makes independent thinking extremely difficult. Conformity leads to mediocrity. To be different from the group or to resist environment is not easy and is often risky as long as we worship success... Education should help us to discover lasting values so that we do not merely cling to*

formulas, or repeat slogans... Education should not encourage the individual to conform to society or to be negatively harmonious with it, but help them to discover the true values, which come with unbiased investigation and self-awareness. When there is no self-knowledge, self-expression becomes self-assertion, with all its aggressive and ambitious conflicts. Education should awaken the capacity to be self-aware and not merely indulge in gratifying self-expression."

If knowledge is equated with power, then ignorance places you in a weaker instead of a stronger position, professionally, personally and, most importantly, financially. To succeed in life you need to cultivate assertiveness in what you believe in, the courage to challenge any odds, the willingness to command what is rightfully due to you, to defy all forms of conventional wisdom, to challenge the status quo with confidence and continually explore more of what you can be.

In life, those who succeed more are those who know better, understand better, see better, do better and become better in society. Education is by far the only sensible starting point for anyone who intends to achieve long lasting fulfilment in life. This is not strictly confined to academic education; it is the further ability to continually empower yourself through acquiring more knowledge by personal development. Knowledge is the only sense that makes all the other five senses function better; it unlocks their infinite power, their creative potential, and bridges any horizons that existed before.

In 2013, Finland, Hong Kong and Singapore were said to have the best education systems in the world. According to research, a great belief exists that education should not impose certain and specific skill-sets but rather should cover a wider spectrum of learning that could facilitate the process of learning for students, emphasising the ideal that education should not only focus on academics but should be the way by which the meaning of life can be taught. Community skills, which help students improve their self-image and natural talents, inculcate empathy for other people. Problem solving using natural talent rather than the rules in a book is also a skill that is nurtured.

The strong thread of these education systems is that they advocate the value of balancing academic and non-academic learning as significant in improving children's wellbeing and happiness in and outside the school environment. Though the education system in Finland may be viewed as unorthodox, it has proven consistently excellent results over the years as measured by the Program for International Student Assessment, which evaluates and compares the performance of schools and education systems worldwide.

Knowledge has the power to transcend all intellectual barriers, to elevate the individual to a state of being where what were once impossibilities can now be seen as necessary breakthroughs. What was once science fiction through the power of knowledge can now become science fact. Through knowledge, humanity has been able to manipulate the principles of nature to fly airplanes and float cargo ships weighing more than a hundred tonnes.

The essence of education is to harness the thinking skills of individuals, to create a conducive environment for them to move in a direction where they can explore their capabilities, to recuperate and rekindle their creative confidence and to open their minds to the self-awareness that their possibilities are unlimited and that they too have the innate ability to use their talents, skills and expertise to make a positive difference in the world. When education ignites this spark in individuals, it serves as a vessel to express the wealth of natural talents in us all and empowers us with a healthy courage and curiosity to question conventional wisdom and to challenge the status quo. It grants us the opportunity to recreate the present and shape the future instead of reiterating yesterday and living the remnants of our past. It is about taking a full responsibility and accountability for your own education, to learn all that you need to learn, develop all the skills you need in order to become the person you want to be and achieve all the things you aspire to have.

Education paves the way and cultivates in people an inherently optimistic outlook of what is possible and how each of us is capable of creating breakthroughs that can catapult society to even greater heights and unlock the potential in the human mind. An education that acts as a key to the treasures of the mind is more often self-education; the innate discipline to stay curious beyond what conventional educational curricula offer and to set out with utter determination to seek more knowledge, more awareness and the expansion of the circumference of one's imagination to unlock breakthrough discoveries.

"Wealth is the product of man's capacity to think."
Ayn Rand

SELF-DISCIPLINE AND CONFIDENCE

"We must let go of our little self, so as to discover our true magnificent self…"

Most people give up even before they try. Yet it is as much effort to lose as it is to win. Self-esteem and self-discipline are the first principles to overcoming fear, which is the barrier to discovering your potential for greatness. Every day presents a new discovery, experience, challenge and opportunity. Most people give up on their dreams even before they try; they lack the personal discipline to stick to the promise they have made to themselves. These are people you cannot trust. The fact that they can't keep a promise they have made to themselves for themselves is enough proof that they cannot keep a promise to anyone.

In pursuit of realising our dreams, we must cultivate in ourselves a self-discipline that allows us to overlook any setbacks. Self-discipline is an everyday process of focusing your mind and heart to your ambitions and striving for them tenaciously so as to achieve them. When you give up on your dream, you give up on yourself; when you give up on yourself, you are giving up on life; when you give up on life, you are basically ceasing to live. Keep the fire in you alive to mould your dreams into reality. The trait of a noble soul and the primary purpose of living is to keep the fire burning to turn dreams into reality. The true measure of greatness is in cultivating an understanding that the courage to pursue a course in life requires that one summons twice as much discipline to see it through, to finish it.

If individuals lacks the persistence, courage, determination and boldness to pursue their life aspirations consistently and aggressively, they lack self-discipline. The lack of self-discipline makes them lose courage along the way. And it is in this lack of self-discipline that you see how such people invest time in discouraging other people who are optimistic about their dreams. It is in this lack of self-discipline that you find such people investing time in excessive drinking, in jobs that do not fulfill them. It is in this lack of self-discipline that all of these people are frustrated, stressed and depressed, with no sense of direction, and spend whole days mourning the world and complaining about everything in it. Such people ought to be so tired of complaining and so sick of not working toward their dreams that they find the medication to cure themselves, and the only medication for this type of sickness is to bring their dreams into reality.

Realising that confidence comes naturally with greatness and greatness comes only to those who are confident is important. Confidence is what you feel about yourself as a result of how you think about yourself. When you sow in your mind high and positive thoughts about yourself, you will reap high and positive feelings about yourself. This greatly determines what you can be and, most importantly what you can do, therefore achieve. So begin every day of your life with a bowl and not a dose of great confidence. Strive to be a success every day. Believe in yourself, believe in your dreams, trust your abilities and have confidence in your potential.

The question I often ask people when they say they are not confident is simple: "Are you confident that you are not confident?".

I often look at a company's vision and think to myself that that is someone else's vision. It might be called a corporate vision because a collection of thousands of people invest their time, energy, intelligence and everything that they have to see that it comes true. The truth is it started as some person's dream which he or she believed in and got other people to believe in, and now the dream has manifested itself as a great company in its industry. The question is, however, by believing in your personal vision as much or even ten times as much as people believe in a company's vision, what do you think can prevent you from realising it? What do you think are the odds of achieving it? Have you the courage and determination to work relentlessly towards your dream? It might not look easy to achieve at first sight, but remember it is not difficult either. Your willingness to constantly strive to make it come true is what counts and makes it worth it at the end of the day.

"I hated every minute of training, but I said, 'Don't quit. Suffer now and live the rest of your life as a champion."
Muhammad Ali

What you do with your *time* will determine your destiny and the achievement. By investing your time in progressively realising your dream, you can look back ten or twenty years from now and realise that your put your efforts, your heart and strength in something that paid off.

By far the most revered currency speculator in the world is George Soros, who lives in a world of speed, high flying big finance, speculations that change the world in milliseconds and the critical significance of a cent, which is what the individual who broke the Bank of England is all about. In his field, accurate decisions with successful investments demand courage, self-discipline and confidence and are the test of true character. On the morning of 16 September 1992, Soros held firmly to his decision and wrote history in the currency-trading world. His firmness in holding to his conviction would later earn him the title of '*The man, who broke the Bank of England*' and, as the story goes, Soros pocketed a profit of $1billion on that one day. His unequivocal confidence in his decision and the discipline to stick to that decision yielded him high returns. Knowing very well he was in a risky business, on that Wednesday at 7:00 a.m. was what Winston Churchill would have called "*His Finest Hour*". As he quips about that memorable event in his life: "At worst, if I had to repay what I had borrowed at the same rate I had borrowed it at, I would have lost at most about 4 percent.

So there was really very little risk involved." This statement epitomises perfectly *amat victoria curam.*

Great achievements in life are dependent upon previous consistent practice and preparation; without such preparation and discipline in hard work there can never be sufficient confidence to take actions that yield immeasurable success. '*By failing to prepare, you are preparing to fail,*' Benjamin Franklin once said. Sometimes opportunities will not knock on your door, which therefore means knocking on as many doors as possible yourself to find that one opportunity that belongs to you. When you finally find something you are passionate about in life, something that allows you to express, embrace and celebrate your talents, hold on to it, grab it with your arms tightly and give your mind, heart and everything to it. Give your all to it, as though your life depends on it, because it really does. Believe in yourself and your dreams. Self-esteem is the state of living in absolute absence of self-doubt. You live once, and if you do it right, then once is enough. Follow your heart, live with passion.

In whatever you do, your purpose and relevance in this world are found at the heart of your talents, gifts and capabilities. In any field or profession, each one's relevance is in his ability to use those gifts to serve other people. This therefore justifies the truth that the fundamental purpose of each person in this world is to enrich the experience of life for others. It is within you to hold in esteem your abilities, potential, talents and gifts. The greatest mistake you can make is to undermine your potential, undervalue your talents, underestimate your abilities and underprice your value. These leads to questioning self-worth and ultimately settling for less than your worth. Self-worth grows when you overvalue, over price your worth in life, and then work hard to reach those standards.

CONFORMITY - Life's Greatest Danger

Over the years I have taken an interest in patterns of human excellence by observing differences between people who are successful and those who are merely breathing. The patterns of distinctions are succinct and I have picked one among them to discuss, in that is *Conformity,* a direct opposite of *Constructive Rebellion.* Conformity by simple definition, is an elusive obligation as a result of social conditioning to compromise your standards and settle for a life less than you are worth. Conformity creates comfort zones, and comfort zones are danger zones; no-go zones. They create complacency and being complacent makes you irrelevant. Comfort zones should make you uncomfortable. In the long run they are a potential discovery trap because they deny you the opportunity to explore more of your life and discover more of what you can truly be.

It has occurred to me that most curious people in society are at least by conventional reasoning the least satisfied. This is partly due to these individuals having discovered that ignorance is not bliss; in fact, it is life's greatest tragedy. People who have established a strong sense of purpose in their lives know that to reach the heights of greatness one must strive to reach the depths of service first. They know that to serve others is the greatest honour that can be bestowed upon any human being. That is why service should be executed with pride and excellence.

Sadly observation shows that innumerable numbers of people in society have become victims of social conditioning, striving to fit in instead of striving to stand out. When you want to make a difference in society you start first by being different. You must recognise that uniformity creates conformity, and conformity is a short cut to mediocrity. Why then try to fit in when you were born to stand out? Why try to be like the other person when you can be the best of you and not end up missing out on the great person that is in front of the mirror?

In my opinion, you may never know what you are capable of until you try. You will never touch the sky until you dare to fly. Reach for the stars, and if you ever fall, fall on the moon; however, if you are going to safely land, then land in the reality of your dreams. You have only one lifetime and as you make the best out of it, then once is enough. Refuse to be trapped in dogma, living other people's ethos. Stop beating yourself down by looking down on your true self. Cheer yourself up and embrace your uniqueness and authenticity. That is what the world wants from you.

There is no virtue in modesty. Live your life to its fullest, express your potential to its optimum and celebrate your talent to its greatest. You are here and here now for a special reason, to serve a special purpose in the world. Do not waste your time following other people's rules; those rules are yellow lines on the road that leads to their destiny, not yours. Refuse to live by someone else's standards, set your own standards for your life. When you measure yourself against someone else's standards, you will always come out second. Do not fall into someone else's plan, and you know why? Because they have nothing much planned for you. Your life is your own book and you should write your own success story — do not allow someone to hold the pen for you.

Avoid at all costs finding yourself in a comfort zone; continually strive to catapult yourself into your success zone. Do not be like the rest; strive to be the best at what you were born to be. The only rule to being an exception to the rule is to not play by the rules. Have a sense of *chutzpah* — the boldness, courage, assertiveness and the audacity to command with your presence — to continually question conventional wisdom and challenge the status quo. At the ocean you find surfers riding the waves. However, the surfer can only enjoy surfing when there is a wave and the wave can only be there because of the winds. The wave in this instance symbolises a trend. The surfer is the trend follower and the wind is the trendsetter. The question is this: are you the surfer or the wind? Are you the trendsetter or the trend follower? Strive to be the wind. Never conform, never try to fit in and be careful whose rules you follow. When it comes to your life and aspirations, remember that your opinion of yourself remains fact. Do not let other people's opinion of you become your reality. When it comes to achieving your goal it's your way or the high way and, quite frankly, you own the highway too.

"Lack of self-confidence, sometimes alternating with unrealistic dreams of heroic success, often leads to procrastination, and many studies suggest that procrastinators are self-handicappers; rather than risk failure, they prefer to create conditions that make success impossible, a reflex that of course creates a vicious circle."

James Surowiecki

PURPOSE AND TALENTS

It is not your current situation in life that will determine how successful you become in life; it is your attitude towards your current situation that will most definitely determine how successful you are in your future. Some people have a prosperity mindset and others a scarcity mindset. Often the people with the prosperity mindset change their circumstances in life to suit their strengths and ability to seize opportunities. They see opportunity in everything and they make the best of it. As for those with a scarcity mindset, believe that there just isn't enough out there for everyone and they use their circumstances against themselves. This is a solvable puzzle!

Then again, the problem about having a problem in your life is that it's always difficult to find a solution, especially when you can't figure out the cause of the problem. So whatever you think of as a problem in your life right now, think of it as a temporary situation. By seeing it as a situation, you are changing your Attitude towards your circumstances and becoming more objective and opportunistic. When you think of your circumstances as problems, you often try to find a way around them, which is a problem itself. And when you think of your circumstances as a temporary situation, then you try to find your way through them and make the best out of them.

Whatever situation you are in right now, think of it as an opportunity to discover your strengths, blessings and gifts. Ask yourself, 'What am I learning and how can I use this current situation as a stepping stone to realise my own dreams?" Try not to use your current circumstances in life *against* yourself, rather use them *for* yourself, as fuel to propel you forward toward realising your dreams and purpose in life.

People have a habit that has evolved into second nature — they look down on their capabilities and talents and look up on other people's capabilities and talents. It is almost as if they look at themselves in the mirror and quickly conclude that they are not good enough; they don't have what it takes. They bite themselves, they trample on themselves, and they even invite the world to push them down, as if they haven't already done enough damage by themselves.

Our talents and capabilities are a gift. They are expressions of immeasurable love for the world through us, so failure to pursue our talents and be the best at them means failure to carry that message to the world, and failure to have served our purpose for living. The truth is, when it comes to what we can do and what we can achieve, only we have the power to set the limits upon ourselves. Everyone is blessed with the ability to be whatever they want to be in this life. You can be whatever you want to be, despite the limits each of us has to our capabilities and achievements. You can be as much of a success as you want; unfortunately, you can also be as much a loser as you want to be. All is in your hands.

So whatever you think of yourself, whether you think you can't, whether you think you can, either way you are right and the choice is yours. The truth about talents and abilities is that although we are blessed with them at birth, they are hardly, if ever, inherited. These gifts are harnessed mostly by exploring them, being around people who share similar talents, who are more experienced, more refurbished, and their energies will rub on to you. What they have learned and their works will inspire your talents and direct you to success.

Our talents and abilities are treasures like any other natural resource that has value to the world; however, talents and abilities do not come on a silver platter to us. We have to work hard on ourselves. Like natural resources that have to be dug from deep in the ground, then put outside of the earth, washed, processed through great heat and chemicals, our talents and capabilities are the same; we have to dig deep into ourselves, work hard on ourselves every day, practising our skills, acquiring consistently more knowledge and information to constantly sharpen and harness them.

Developing these inborn elements in us requires great effort, time and energy to work at them until they are fine-tuned and outstanding. The Beatles, for instance, although talented and capable musicians, had to work at their skills every day, practising tirelessly and diligently, spending countless hours doing so before they had their first hit single in 1969. Tiger Woods, the greatest golfer of our time, practised his golf from as early as the age of three, and even today, to stay at the top, Tiger Woods practices his swings and moves every day. Therefore the development of our talents and capabilities requires daily commitment to them.

We all have a unique talent that we ought to offer to the world. We ought also to stay true to ourselves, educate ourselves more by taking interest in things that fascinate our imagination and ignite the fire within us to be better. We ought to cautiously stay away from people who bring us down and laugh at our dreams. The moment we treat ourselves benevolently and give some value and respect to the uniqueness of the people around us, we give to the world something that no one can take from us, something that is our gift to the world - our true selves.

THE STORY OF GILLIAN LYNNE BY SIR KEN ROBINSON

In his enlightening book *The Element – How Finding your Passion Changes Everything*, Sir Ken Robinson directs us to the story of 89 year-old Gillian Barbara Lynne, DBE, who is a world renowned British ballerina, dancer, actor, theatre and television director and choreographer. Gillian is still as passionate and vibrant about ballet and the arts as she was when she was only eight years old. Her story epitomises what happens when one seeks one's passion in life, finds it and makes a living out of it. As the saying goes, do what you love and love what you do. It is then safe to conclude that for the past eight decades Gillian has never worked. And how is that? She does what she loves for a living.

Born in 1926 in the United Kingdom, just two years before the Great Depression, when passion and talent were not a luxury to fantasise about, when everyone was thinking about where to get the next meal. Gillian's early life was a nightmare. She was not a bubbly or energetic child scoring straight As. Her school life was a complete disaster, a world of hopelessness, and she did not know how to escape it. She would very often turn her work in late, her handwriting was unimpressive even for an eight year old, not that they have impressive handwriting at that age, and she barely passed her class tests, putting her at the bottom of the academic pyramid.

A restless child with a low concentration span, she tried to keep some excitement in her daily life and, be curious about the world out there, where deep within she felt she belonged, Gillian sometimes stared out of class. While the teacher was doing her job, the child would fidget and disturb the whole class, putting everyone ill at ease and distracting the class. What was wrong with the eight year old? She was behaving entirely differently from all the other kids; she was different and she refused to be like everyone else.

Her restless and distractive behaviour very soon put her in trouble with the school's authority, and eventually the school wrote to her parents, as any of them do when they have run out of tricks to change a child, assuming she was suffering from a learning disorder or, bluntly put, was intellectually impaired. This ignorant assumption led to the school suggesting that Gillian attend a school for children with special needs, as opposed to a school for children with special talents and gifts. In a modern day school, a child similar to Gillian would be labelled an ADHD child, presumably sentencing her to a lifetime of anti-depressants and excruciating medical routines to keep her in check and intact.

Like any loving parents would do, Gillian's parents out of concern sought assistance for their daughter, taking her to see a psychologist for an assessment of her special intellectual condition, as the teachers had suggested. Her parents feared that they would hear the saddest news about their daughter, and no one knew, not even Gillian herself, that she was to have a blind date with her true purpose in life at the psychologist's office. Her parents were worried about hearing overwhelming news about Gillian's condition and possibly shedding a tear, and they did in fact meet with overwhelming news and an epiphany that made them shed tears of joy and begin a life of wonder, joy, fulfilment, success and immeasurable happiness in Gillian's life. The child was freed from the chains of conventional wisdom and the stereotypes of the school system in which she did not entirely belong. On this day, at this place, Gillian became one with her true self, her true identity and, most importantly, her passion, her purpose and her meaning of life. Unlike many people, Gillian was lucky to find her purpose in life very early and receive the right direction to blossom into something that would become the centre of her entire life.

Today, Gillian runs her own company, which teaches ballet. She is also the respectable brains behind 'The Phantom of the Opera', for which she provides musical staging and choreography. She has received multiple global awards for her contribution to the arts, including, among others, the Mr. Abbott Award, the Austrian Silver Order of Merit for her production of 'Cats' in Vienna. She was further honoured by the Royal Academy of Dance with the Queen Elizabeth II Coronation Award; appointed Commander of the Order of the British Empire (CBE) in 1997 and Dame Commander of the Order of the British Empire (DBE) in the 2014 New Year Honours for service to dance and musical theatre.

Looking back to when she was eight and that fateful day with the psychologist, Gillian says in the interview with Sir Ken Robinson that she remembers being invited into a large oak-panelled room with leather-bound books on the shelves. Standing in the room was a man in a tweed jacket. He took her to the far end of the room and sat her down on a huge leather sofa. Her feet didn't touch the floor and swung in the air. Being nervous and told not to fidget, the child sat on her hands. The man in the tweed jacket, who was Gillian's psychologist, went to his desk and for about twenty minutes asked Gillian's mother about her daughter's difficulties at school and the problems she was said to be causing.

After a while Gillian's mother stopping talking and the man rose from his desk and sat close to Gillian, thanking her for her patience. He asked if they could leave her in the room for a few minutes, to which the little girl agreed. As the man was leaving the room, he went to his desk and turned the radio on. As they stood in the corridor, the doctor asked Gillian's mother to watch through the window what Gillian did; in a short while, the little girl was taken by the magic in the music and began moving gracefully around the room. Her graceful flow and movement in response to the music seemed to come naturally and flawlessly to Gillian.

Eventually the psychologist, overwhelmed, turned to Gillian's mother and said, "You know, Mrs. Lynne, Gillian isn't sick. She's a dancer. Take her to a dance school." The mother took the psychologist's advice and enrolled Gillian at a dance school. Gillian's first expression on arriving at the dance school was utter excitement and spiritual relief. "I can't tell you how wonderful it was. I walked into this room, and it was full of people like me. People who couldn't sit still; people who had to move to think."

Gillian went to dance school every week and practised at home every day. In the end, she auditioned for the Royal Ballet School in London and was accepted. She went on to lead a successful career in dancing, joining the Royal Ballet Company, becoming a soloist, and performing all over the world.

Gillian is living proof that whoever said you can't mixed business with pleasure must have been ignorant of the significant complementary nature of the two. She does what she loves and loves what she does. Her pleasure is her business and she has made a success of it and her life with it, personally and professionally as well. When asked at the age of 87 if she will ever retire, she replied:

"I think everybody has to have a purpose in life and the word 'retirement' should be struck off and stamped upon, consigned to deep rivers and flown out to sea because it is a dangerous word and I think every day one needs, when they get up in the morning, they need a purpose to take them through the day. And so I suppose my purpose has always been the craft of theatre. I love theatre."

Although Gillian was labeled an incapable student at a conventional school, she found her strength and talents in dance school, where her genius blossomed. Perhaps when you take a moment to evaluate traits in you labeled as weaknesses, you will realise that your weaknesses are a gateway to inner strengths that you have not yet tapped into. There are no such things as weaknesses, only gateways to hidden strengths. Ludwig van Beethoven, still celebrated today as a musical genius, was partly deaf in his later years, yet it is said that he produced the best classical songs during this period. His partial deafness perhaps helped increase his inner sense of hearing. Because he was not able to hear sounds from outside, he heard the music playing in his heart and experienced the joy and elevation of spirit it brought to him in sharp acuity in the chambers of his soul.

His partial deafness helped protect him from the distractions of the sounds of the outside world, allowing him to focus more on his inner strength, the ability to create authentic music that resonated from deep within him. In Mary Oliver's poem 'The Journey', she writes, "But little by little, as you left your voices behind, the stars began to burn through the sheets of clouds and there was a new voice which you slowly recognised as your own that kept you company as you strode deeper and deeper into the world, determined to do the only thing you could do -- determined to save the only life you could save."

Perhaps if Beethoven had not been partially deaf, he would have been unable to hear and write the wonderful songs that played deep within him and needed to be composed and shared with the world. Today, he is still celebrated as one of the greatest classical music composers of all time. Possibly our weaknesses distract us and keep us from focusing on our inner strengths. By trying to understand our weaknesses, we realise their value and importance in our lives and their purpose of sharpening our inner strengths.

Many people are unaware that they are worth more than the price tag they have stuck on their foreheads. Their talents are the wealth that they bring with them to this world to enrich the experience of life for others and make the world a better place than the one they found. When you invest in your talents, you discover that passion, creativity and boundless energy come naturally when you are in your element. Gillian's life proves true that the easiest and fastest way to be successful in this world is to make a living by serving others through your talents, while doing something you are passionate about. This is the simplest way to be relevant and make a positive difference in the world.

DISCOVERING YOUR PURPOSE

In each one of us lies a purpose for this world, a special reason why we are here and a purpose to fulfill with our lives. Our duty is to seek and find that purpose and then use it to serve those around us, to make this world a better place, as it is intended to be. When you establish a sense of purpose in your life, you find fulfilment and clarity in everything you do. Life takes on a completely different meaning, which makes you more alive and helps you rekindle your creative confidence because you are in your element.

By dedicating your life to a definite course, one which gives you a complete sense of joy, fulfilment and true expression of your abilities and talents, you have taken a stand to lead a purpose-driven life. Waking up every day you know that what you live for is something that is bigger than you and yet positively beneficial to society and people. Life becomes beautiful when you realise that you have more to give to this world and make it a better place through serving it with your talents and gifts. The greatest joy of life comes through giving freely and happily of your talents to the world. You know then that the world is gradually becoming a better place because you are giving it what it needs the most, the best of yourself.

Discovering your purpose is often atemporal and naturally has a satori effect; it is like looking for your car keys, only to find that they were actually in your pocket the whole time. Your purpose in life naturally expresses itself through your talents. Purpose is talent given meaning through service in life. When you discover what you are truly gifted at, something that you seem to have a naturally high aptitude for, be it mathematics, music, science, arts, athletics, writing or drawing; just as the fish thrives in water, the eagle in the sky, the seeds in the earth, you also have your way with something in this world, it's your element.

Then right there your purpose has given you a clue what it is; it is that which makes your heart sing. It is that one skill that resonates with your inner spirit that ignites your enthusiasm and is reflective of your true personality and character. Each of us thrives at something, and the harder we work at it, the more we know we can become great at it. We have a sense of *sprezzatura* for it, according to Baldassare Castiglione. There is just a natural flow of positive energy and boundless creativity when we do it. It is an ability that seems to come to you naturally, seamlessly and without any effort whatsoever.

Your talents in life are gifts to the world through you. They are a way to communicate the beauty of his *LOVE* to the world through you. We are all here for the sake of others, to serve them with who we are and the talents bestowed upon us. Life is a miracle; discovering and honouring your purpose is how you celebrate it. Purpose is when you give meaning and relevance to your talents by making a living out of them through serving others. Each and every one of us is born with a purpose to make this world a better place in some way and through our talents we fulfill this promise.

"All the powers in the universe are already ours. It is we who have put our hands before our eyes and cry that it is dark."

Swami Vivekananda

Setting Audacious Goals

"Be cautionary and strategic, understand the position you are in and work steadily and relentlessly towards your goals."

Aim high, shoot straight. They say you can never score unless you have a goal. How daring are your goals? Many of us set goals for ourselves, personally and professionally. The question however is, Are they Audacious enough? It is not about the fabricated SMART goals often relayed in the many corporate settings. I'm referring to brave and boundary transcending goals that pique conventional wisdom, challenge the status quo, set higher standards and change the landscape of the gameplan.

On the 6th May 1954, a historic event took place during a meet between British AAA and Oxford University at Iffley Road Track in Oxford. An audacious goal was set and a new record broken. A young athlete, Roger Bannister would break a world record, setting even high standards for his successor athletes to challenge the rather '*close to impossible*' to record. He became the first ever athlete to break the 1 mile run in less than 4 minutes; 3 minutes 59.4 seconds to be precise! The thought of any human being ever breaking this record was labelled, '*Impossible*' even by Sports physicians and experts. It was an unbreakable rule an unbendable law.

However, Roger wrote history, he achieved the Impossible. What exactly did he do differently in order to turn this limit into a transcendable boundary? He thought differently... His strategy and approach was different. When every athlete thought of breaking the 1 mile record in 4 minutes, Roger thought of breaking the 1 mile record in less than '*240 seconds*'. He changed his focus from minutes into seconds, calculating his run time by seconds as he practiced, every second became an improvement that moved him closer to his goal. Every mistake he transformed into a valuable lesson learned and every failure to beat the record was not a setback instead it was a valuable feedback to him of which he could improve upon. Day by day, second by second he witnessed his improvement from being a victim of the old limiting belief to transforming into a victor of an empowering belief.

Within the next forty six days after this historic event, John Landy broke that record by 3 min 57.9 s and many other athletes began breaking the 4 minute-mile run. But what did Roger really do? He broke the myth, he pushed up the benchmark and set a new trend. He send out an inspiration and an extended invitation not only to athletes but to everyone in their own fields to 'Aim high and shoot straight,'

This chapter is about reminding you about your audacious goals, inspiring you to think differently and do things differently in order to achieve outstanding results. Reminding you to look beyond the boundaries you had set for yourself and dare to rise above the limits you had imposed upon yourself. Empowering you to stand up and do outstanding things in and with your life. It is about motivating you to; Dare to dream and Dare to do it, because you have all the talent, means, expertise and might to achieve whatever the goals you have set for yourself.

World Champion of Public Speaking (1995) Mark Brown once said;

"If you don't do outstanding things in your field of expertise, you will end up standing out alone in the field."

Therefore refuse to give up on our goals or to settle for anything less than what you know you are capable of. Knowing that we can only grow by growing others and the best way to grow others is to set audacious goals for ourselves and achieve outstandingly to inspire others to reach out for more and be more in their own lives too. By each and every one of us holding up our own torch of inspiration and using it as lantern to guide others in finding their own torches, we are making the world a better place one day at a time. Set daring goals and strive to achieve them. While being thankful and grateful never be satisfied with where you are today, continue to stretch yourself further to where you can be tomorrow. Always remember that the road to success is always under construction and the journey in itself is the reward…

'A person without goals is like a sailor with a boat but nowhere to go, no destiny.'

Not having goals is like shooting for the stars blindfolded; you will hit nothing except your foot in the end. Without goals in life, no one would know where to go, what to do, and perhaps even who to be. The goals we have set for ourselves shape our character, which shapes our future and thus shapes our achievements in life.

When setting goals for yourself, it is crucial to understand your current position — your current strengths, weaknesses and, most importantly, the opportunities that seem to avail themselves. Weaknesses can be a great source of strength, provided they are acknowledged and leveraged to yield greater strength. Remember that nothing in life, no goal in life, has ever been too great to be achieved, and that anyone who dares to say your goal, is beyond achievement is not worth being around.

Most people operate out of fear of disappointment; they end up setting lower goals and hence standards, for themselves. Each individual is born with a potential for great achievements within them; however, it is the hard work of bringing those achievements to life that people seem to not want to do. It is in everyone to succeed. The natural personal power we are born with is to set high goals and achieve them.

Set goals for yourself that frighten you, excite you, and raise your expectations about yourself, because anything that moves you from your comfort zone leads you to greater spiritual fulfilment and self-discovery that if not for that great goal would not be felt. Start by setting smaller goals, working towards achieving them, for greatness is built like a house, brick on brick. As you summon the confidence to achieve these goals, set even bigger goals and achieve them, sooner or later you will be astonished at what you have achieved in a short time.

"When you want something, and you want it bad enough, you will always find a way to get it."
Jim Rohn

Most people set goals and sit down and do nothing about achieving them, they expect that some great accident will occur and their goals will be achieved with little or no effort. In trying to avoid challenges that they might encounter, such people wish the challenges were easier, instead of wishing they had more courage, more skills and more abilities to overcome those mere challenges and emerge victorious in their pursuits.

There is a worthwhile saying, 'Reach out for the sky. You may not catch it but you will most certainly catch a shooting star and when you do catch that star, grab it tightly, hold on to it forever, because it will serve as your guiding light to your dreams, your ambitions, your purpose for living and, most importantly, your destiny.'

"The person who makes a success of living is the one who sees their goal steadily and aims for it unswervingly. That is dedication."
Cecil B. De Mille

As long as your focus is as sharp as a whisper through a needle's hole, then your goal is not far-fetched from your target. Everything in this world has an end-goal. In football the goal of both teams is to score more goals than their opponents. The primary purpose of the whole match is to net as many scores as possible in the goal posts. Without a goal, the fundamental purpose of doing something completely loses meaning. Can you imagine soccer players on the field playing without goal posts? The whole purpose of the sport would fade. Each person has goals of some sort, because they give you a reason to jump out of bed in the morning and use your energy, passion and intellect for a worthwhile pursuit.

Everything is goal-orientated; having goals that ignite the fire in you to strive for something that is fulfilling to you is merely a signal that your life's integral trait is to have goals. All purpose in life is shaped around a goal of some sort. The only reason people work hard is because their end goal is to achieve a certain level of greatness in their life, material or immaterial. When you build a blueprint in your mind of your goals, you pave the way for clarity on how you want to use your time and energies and where to direct them.

A guided missile cannot hit any target unless that target has been set for it. Although it might go in a meandering fashion, the fact that its goal has been made clear and stored in its radar sensors serves as a blueprint and guides it where it must ultimately hit. People with clearly defined goals always seem to move in the right direction, and the reason is because they have set in their minds the right destiny, allowing them to gear all their resources toward this meaningful end-goal. Every journey has a destiny; otherwise it would not be a journey but a meaningless go-around-the-circle adventure. Goals give meaning to the journey.

SINGLE-MINDEDNESS OF PURPOSE

Obstacles are those temporary stumbles we tend to see the moment we take our eyes off the goals we have set for ourselves to achieve. Sometimes it is situations you find yourself in or the people around you who are there for a greater purpose and reason. You should realise that how you see them may help you get what you desire in life and where you want to be or where you hate to be. People around you and situations at hand are there to help you get to where you want to get. Life makes way for those ambitious, endearing souls who push boldly against all odds and obstacles.

Most people tend to define success in their lives by the cars, houses, financial wealth or other material possessions; often oblivious to the reality that those possessions are not the actual success, they are referential symbols of success. Success does not begin upon acquisition of these possessions; it is those possessions that are a reward or an outcome of success. When you have set your mind and heart on a definite goal in life, you are already on a success path.

Today he is the CEO of a Fortune 500 company at the tender age of 21. Bill McDermott had flair, ambition and the drive to push himself to the limits and become a successful and respectable person in society and in the world. Bill grew up in Amityville, in the Great South Bay of Long Island. Coming from a modest family and having attended a local C school, Bill carved himself a future and career that all hard-working and determined people can achieve.

His breakthrough came in the mid-seventies when he landed his first job at the age of twenty at Xerox as a copy machine salesman. Taking a stroll down memory lane in his interview about his rise to become head of a Fortune 500 Company, Bill still vividly remembers his job interview and how by the close of that rigorous day he wore the badge of victory and triumph on his chest. Do you still remember your first job interview?

On the morning of the day he went for that first ever interview, rain poured outside and water flooded his house. His brother, proud of his younger brother's move into the corporate jungle, threw him on his shoulder and carried him out of the house so he could board his father's car to take him to the interview. Wearing his new $99 suit, energised and inspired to take his big day by its horns, he promised his father, "Dad, I guarantee you tonight, I'm coming with my employee badge in my pocket." His father, proud of his young son, replied to Bill's promise and said, "Hey, Bill, just do your best. Don't put that kind of pressure on yourself. You're a great guy and I'll be just as proud of you no matter what happens." Bill still vehemently insisted upon his promise to his father and said firmly, "I guarantee you."

On his way to Xerox, Bill took time to read the company's Annual Report just to get a feel of the mammoth he would be arm-wrestling that day and how much he would have to flex his muscles. In that Annual Report, he learned of the then CEO of Xerox, David Kearnes, and was inspired by how much the CEO was driven to change things and turn his organisation into the most innovative player in its industry.

Through numerous interviews that day, his last one for the day started late in the evening, and Bill patiently waited for the interviewer, still inspired and motivated, just as excited in his last interview as he was in the first one of the day, Bill kept his hunger alight for this opportunity that would be a platform for him to shoot straight into the stars. He asked the administrative assistant to assure Mr. Fullwood, the interviewer, who was caught in a meeting, that he shouldn't hurry, he would wait for him regardless of how late it might be. "Joanna, I just want you to please let Mr. Fullwood know that I'm in no rush and I'll be here as late as he needs me to be. I just want him know that I will wait for him and I'll be here as late as he needs me to be for this interview."

Later on that evening, Bill confidently went through his last interview for the day with Mr. Fullwood. At the end of the interview Mr. Fullwood thanked him for his time and the great interview and advised him that the HR Department would be in touch with him in a few weeks. Having set a clear goal for himself and a promise to his father, Bill asked Mr. Fullwood, "Well, Mr. Fullwood, I think there's something that you don't completely understand. I haven't broken a promise to my father in 21 years and I guaranteed him I'd be home tonight with my employee badge in my pocket and I can't let my dad down." Mr. Fullwood, after hearing this very clear and inspiring message, then advised Bill that as long as he hadn't committed any crimes, then he was hired. With a glimmer of excitement in his eyes Bill asked, "I have not committed any crimes, Mr. Fullwood, so could you please repeat that again? Does that mean I'm hired?"

The rest is history and today Bill McDermott is the author of the New York Times bestselling memoir, *Winners Dream; A Journey from Corner Store to Corner Office,* the CEO of SAP SE, a Fortune 500 enterprise software company with a global footprint and an annual turnover in excess of $20 billion that helps large and small organisations run better with their technology.

From an early age Bill knew what he wanted; he had a clear goal in life and a strategy on how he would get there. His fuelled passion became his driving force, a trait he still portrays even 30 years later after his Xerox interview. He says about success, "I think I've always had this really high appreciation for work and what it means to have success and not to take it for granted but just to recognise that success is relative and it comes in every different form and it's completely personal to the individual. But when you taste it, it's just the sweet nectar of life, man. There's just something about it."

"When I went for my first interview at Xerox, I knew exactly what I was there for, I was interviewing for my dream job…they went to interview for a sales job. I went to be the next CEO."

Bill Mcdermott

In every given situation in whatever you do or want to be in life, it is a necessary requirement to cultivate the habit of setting goals for yourself. In any given sport, you will often hear the coach say to his team, 'Keep your eye on the ball at all times.'

"Singleness of purpose is one of the chief essentials for success in life, no matter what may be one's aim."

John D. Rockefeller

Establishing well-formed objectives requires an ability to create an outcome with congruence in your mind, heart and spirit, all converging towards achieving a single goal. When you cultivate the mental discipline of synchronising all your mental energies towards a single objective, you put yourself in a position to achieve phenomenal results. The sheer ability to sharpen your mind's focus and concentrate it towards one goal, eliminating any possible distractions and focusing only on the possibility of hitting your target's bull's eye is mental discipline necessary to achieve outstanding feats.

In establishing a goal that is worthwhile to yourself and worth achieving, it is imperative to put the right conditions in place to enable your mental energy to be directed towards it. The key is to evaluate the state of mind you need in order to achieve the goal. This means organising your internal and external behaviours to elicit the necessary motivation to start. Putting in place the right conditions means stating your goal in a more specific and positive manner; for instance, instead of saying, "I want to lose weight," which has a negation that forces you to picture yourself as overweight before even trying to lose weight, a process which could inhibit the desired outcome, try saying, "I want to be slimmer, in fact 10 kg slimmer, in the next six months."

Any goal is easy to achieve as long as it is within the locus of your control. Do you have full control over the achievement of that goal and have the necessary resources at your disposal to achieve it? Evaluate what measures you need to have in place to track the progress towards achieving it and then break down the tasks into manageable sizes where your achievement of the goal can be incremental and gradual. Most importantly, establish what exactly you will gain ultimately by achieving this goal. People may say they want to be slimmer so that they can gain more confidence in themselves. This means being slimmer is not an end goal for them, it is a means to an end goal, and their actual end goal is having more confidence by being slimmer.

By defining the conditions necessary to enable the achievement of the goal and outlining the steps you need to take, you create a conducive mental and physical ability to achieve the goal. When the mind focuses on a single goal for a long term, it builds a mental blueprint of it and then organises your resources and directs the psychical aspects of your body to achieving it.

To achieve a goal, bear in your mind and heart that there is no set path. You create the path by taking the first bold step. Lead your life, lead your way to the goals you have set for yourself.

"If you chase two rabbits, you will catch neither one of them."
Russian Proverb

DEMYSTIFYING FEAR

"Face your fears with all confidence, for behind all your fears lies your greatest strengths and abilities."

Fear is a natural response you get when you move closer to something that is great, your true self. By living through your fears you give yourself the opportunity to claim your power although it is a disempowering response elicited by a false sense of who you really are and capable of achieving. It signals the use of one's creative imagination in a negative way to create elusive overly exaggerated images in your mind, which are later mistaken for reality. Our perception of reality is often not a true reflection of reality but a reflection of our own state of mind. We create pictures in our minds and then become a victim of them. The walls that you see around you that seem to inhibit you from discovering your true potential actually only exist in your mind, not in reality.

Fear is a misinterpretation of positive anticipation. Often fear is given the acronym **F**alse **E**vidence **A**ppearing **R**eal. Fear has robbed many people of their dreams and has incarcerated many people's potential to discover their real worth. The truth is that there is nothing to be afraid of. In fact there is every reason to become the best you know truly from the bottom of your heart that you can be.

Everyone does not fear the reality of their dreams; however, they fear the illusions they have created in their minds of failure. People invest much time in the day building pictures in their minds of why they will not succeed and why they will not dare to even try to succeed. Being controlled by fear is no different in my opinion from a dog being wagged by its own tail. Fear is similar to what happens when a mountaineer looks at a molehill and sees Mount Everest. Courage, in the opposite way, is what happens when a mountaineer looks at Mount Everest, sees a molehill and realises that he has all the resources and abilities required to reach the top. When you plague your mind with thoughts of fear, it is natural then that all you will see and all you will be is the sum total of your daily fears.

People do not fear that which they know, or that which is alive, people fear that which they have created in their minds. They cultivate and harness thoughts of fear in their minds until fear comes naturally to them. Fear is what we feel, what we cultivate in us, when our desire and determination to pursue our goals and achieve our dreams is outweighed by self-doubt. We perpetuate thoughts of fear in ourselves until we become immobile in pursuit of our aspirations as a result of the fears we have created in our own minds. Fear is a toxic element to the mind. The more of it in the mind, the less a person becomes in life. They are afraid to take the first wrong step that will lead them to the second right step. The truth is people fear to take the first step, but what shocks me is how little fear people have to sit and do nothing about their dreams.

Although many people sit every day, dreaming about being successful, they hardly take the first step, and their reasoning is that it is risky. The biggest risk that people accept in each day is the risk of not pursuing their life's aspirations and ambitions. By not pursuing their dreams, they risk all the greatness, fulfilment, and joy that would come with their dreams being realised. They risk all that in exchange for doing nothing, just complaining about the way things are instead of making things the way they should be. When you set out on a path that leads to the attainment of your goals, you do not become a risk taker. Instead you become an adventure seeker; so explore and enjoy the thrill of doing something new and exciting in your life that will help you grow.

When your fear for the known past outweighs your fear for the unknown future, it becomes easier to summon enough courage and faith to march forward boldly.

To allow one's fears to conquer you is to live a life of misery, loss and worthlessness; to conquer one's fears is to live a victorious, fulfilling and happy life. When you don't have fear for the unknown, the unknown will be kind to you. Most people are either merely content or accepting of a life of fear; however, a few and all-successful people have conquered their own fears. They realise that deep in nature every individual is blessed with an infinite power to control and possess their own minds and direct it to the ends which they desire.

Like success, fear is a state of mind, therefore is cultivated. The more one's thoughts are invested in fear, the more fear grows. The more fear grows, the more it takes on a life of its own and dominates all the faculties of the mind until they surrender to it. We allow fear to live in us by constantly entertaining thoughts that embody it, by surrounding ourselves with people who have cultivated it in acres in their minds, and by finding in all situations that we may fear.

It is yet an overlooked truth that at the heart of fear, at the centre of it, lie the greatest abilities in us we could ever have imagined. It is a relieving truth that fear is vulnerable and helpless. It seeks comfort in us and grows as we provide much of it. We embrace and nourish it until it becomes so powerful it controls us; yet we harnessed it and planted it in our hearts and minds like a seed and grew it by watering it every day with thoughts that warmed it like sunshine. We bear our own fears in us, we create them, we nourish them, until they shadow us, until we submit to them, until they make us something we never wanted to be.

ALLEGORY OF THE CAGE

The characters below are fictitious; they are merely used to convey the message.

[**The Eagle**] And now let me show you in a figure how far our nature is enlightened or unenlightened. Behold! Five birds locked in a cagewhich has a gate open towards the sky and reaching above; they have been in there from their birth, and have their legs and wings locked in a cage so that they cannot fly and can only see before them, being prevented by the cage from flapping their wings and flying into the sky.

[**The Sparrow**] I see.

[**The Eagle**] And do you see birds locked in a cage, they cannot fly, they cannot reach out into the sky, and they are not free to be in their true nature.

[**The Sparrow**] You have shown me a strange image, and they are strange prisoners.

[**The Eagle**] Like ourselves, and they see only the sky, the trees and the far out stars and galaxies.

[**The Sparrow**] True how could they be anything but the locked birds if they were never allowed to flap their wings and fly?

[**The Eagle**] And of the objects, which are being carried in like manner, they would only see the sky but not explore?

[**The Sparrow**] Yes.

[**The Eagle**] And if they were able to converse with one another, would they not suppose that they were being denied the ability to explore their true nature?

[**The Sparrow**] Very true.

[**The Eagle**] And suppose further that the birds had an echo which came from the other side. Would they not be sure to fancy to fly with one of the free birds that flew over the cage?

[**The Sparrow**] No question.

[**The Eagle**] To them the truth would be literally nothing but the objects of which they should be.

[**The Sparrow**] That is certain.

[**The Eagle**] And now look again and see what will naturally follow if the birds are released and disabused of the error. At first, with any being liberated and compelled suddenly to fly into the sky and see the light, it will suffer sharp pains; the glare will distress it, and it will be unable to see the realities of which in its former state it had felt imprisoned; and they conceive another bird saying to it that what it saw before was an illusion, but that now, with its approaching nearer to being and its eye turned towards more real existence, it has a clearer vision, — what will be its reply? And you may further imagine that its instructor is pointing to the sky as they pass and requiring it to name it — will the beauty not perplex it? Will it not fancy that imprisonment in which it formerly lived as truer than the beauty of the sky which is now shown to it?

[**The Sparrow**] Far truer

[**The Eagle**] And if it is compelled to look straight into the sky, will it not have a pain in its eyes which will make it turn away to take and take in its objects of vision which it can see and which it will conceive to be in reality clearer than the things which are now being shown to it?

[**The Sparrow**] True, it is now.

[**The Eagle**] And suppose once more that it is reluctantly dragged up a steep and rugged ascent, and it will fly fast until it's forced into the presence of the sun itself, is it not likely to be pained and irritated? With its, approaches the light in its eyes will be dazzled, and it will not be able to see anything at all of what are now called realities.

[**The Sparrow**] Not all in a moment.

[**The Eagle**] It will require you to grow accustomed to this sight of its upper world. And first it will see its shadows best, next its reflections of other birds and the world below it, the water; it will gaze upon the light of the sun and the stars; and it will see the sky and the stars by night better than the sun or the light of the sun by day?

[**The Sparrow**] Certainly.

[**The Eagle**] Last will it be able to see the beauty of the sky and not mere imaginations of it, but will see it in its own proper place and not through the bars of the cage and contemplate it as it is?

[**The Sparrow**] Certainly

[**The Eagle**] Will it then proceed to argue that this is it which gives the season and the years and is the guardian of all that is in the visible world, and in a certain way the cause of all things which it and its fellow birds have been accustomed to behold?

[**The Sparrow**] Clearly, it would first see the skies and the reason about it.

[**The Eagle**] And with it remembering its old habitation and the wisdom of the cage and its fellow-prisoners, do you not suppose that it would felicitate itself on the change and pity them?

[**The Sparrow**] Certainly, it would.

[**The Eagle**] And if it were in the habit of conferring honours among themselves on those who were quickest to observe the passing shadows of other birds and to remark which of them went before and which followed after and which were together and who were therefore best able to draw conclusions as to the future, do you think that it would care for such honours and glories, or envy the possessors of blue skies? Would it not say with Homer?

Better to be the great servant of a great master,

And to endure anything, rather than think as they do and live after their manner?

[**The Sparrow**] Yes, I think that it would rather suffer anything than entertain these false notions and live in this miserable manner.

[**The Eagle**] Imagine once more such a one coming suddenly out of the sky to be replaced in its old situation, would it not be certain to have its eyes full of darkness?

[**The Sparrow**] To be sure.

[**The Eagle**] And if there were a contest and the bird had to compete in measuring the beauty of the skies with the imprisoned birds who had never moved out of the cage, while its sight was still weak, and before its eyes and wings had become steady (and the time which would be needed to acquire its new habit of sight might be very considerable) would it not be ridiculous? Other birds would say of it that up it went and up it came without its eyes; and that it was better not even to think of ascending; and if any one tried to lose another and fly into the skies, let one catch the offender and they would put it to death.

[**The Sparrow**] No question.

[**The Eagle**] This entire allegory, you may now append the sparrow to the previous argument; the prison-house or cage is your fears, the bird is your dreams, ambitions and aspirations, and you will not misinterpret me if you interpret the journey upwards to be the realisation of your dreams and ambitions. Setting yourself free from your fears to ascend to greater achievements and personal discovery according to my poor belief, which, at your desire, I have expressed with the rightly or wrongly. But, with the true or false, my opinion is that in the world of knowledge the idea of good appears last of all, and is seen only with an effort; and, with being seen, is also inferred to be the universal author of all things beautiful and right, parent of light and of the lord of light in this visible world, and the immediate source of reason and truth in the intellectual; and that this is the power upon which it who would act rationally, either in public or private life in pursuit of their dreams must have their eye, heart and mind fixed to it, to achieve it.

[**The Sparrow**] I agree as far as I am able to understand you.

[**The Eagle**] Moreover you must not wonder that those who attain to this beatific vision are unwilling to descend to birdy affairs; for their souls are ever hastening into the upper world with desire to dwell; with a desire of great success which is very natural if our allegory may be trusted.

[**The Sparrow**] Yes, very natural.

The birds in this allegory symbolise an individual's aspirations, dreams and ambitions while the cage represents the fears that people have of realising these dreams.

Message of this allegory; your fears are a bridge, a gateway to your talents and strengths. The day you stop having fear for the unknown, the unknown will be kind to you. You will realise that the unknown, which is the future, is dependent upon you to give it shape and meaning with your ambition, imagination and talents. *Fear in itself is not the absence of courage; it is the shadow of courage. So why hide in the shadow when you can rise into the light of your courage? It is in the light of courage that your dreams shine and you discover the greatness in you.*

We all have dreams, ambitions and aspirations; we all want to achieve more and become more. We have a burning desire to make our mark in this world; we have things we would like to achieve and show to the world. However, we dwell, comfortably, in our fears. We nestle our dreams in our fears and never challenge ourselves to bring our dreams into reality. We make fear our dearest friend instead of seeing it as our worst enemy.

Fear is what we have, what we feel, when the desire, passion and determination to pursue our life's aspirations are outweighed by self-doubt. Most people are not living their dreams and might never reach them if they continue living their fears. Fear is, in fact, a creative thought couched in negative form instead of positive. It is merely imagined impossibilities. It does not exist until you create it, harness it and empower it by believing in it and its possibility — you give it life. Then you in awareness or unawareness take actions that manifest it. Your fears are just as real as the power you inject in them by the belief you put in them; otherwise there is nothing to fear, only your fears themselves.

What you fear in life your mind often unconsciously gravitates to; by mere virtue of thinking about it, thinking it through, visualising it, you create an environment for it to exist. Your fears are distorted visions of your mind. According to Professor Albert Bandura, people are active information processors and always try to make sense of the relationship between their behaviour and its consequences. People learn by either experience or observation. If the people around them are afraid of snakes, they will most likely also be afraid of snakes even if snakes had not harmed them previously at all.

Fear is like a dark cloud that cloaks your soul; it is like a poison that contaminates your thoughts. It is a smoke that blinds you from seeing the greatness and abundance within you to manifest your true capabilities. Fear only exists in the mind that creates it. Without that thought it would not exist, just as there would be no act without an actor. It is a liability to a healthy mind, it is like a virus that enters the mind and then breeds endlessly until the mind that carries it becomes its own victim. Any virus multiplies when it finds a warm place with nutrients that allow it to breed. Fear is nurtured by belief.

Professor Albert Bandura's theory of guided mastery outlines an interesting scientific process on how he helped his patients overcome the fear of snakes by modelling behaviour, increasing the patient's self-efficacy and proficiency. His idea was that unless people believe that they can achieve a particular desired outcome by their actions, they have little incentive to act and persevere in the face of any difficulties.

One reason people often use a fraction of their potential is because they are mentally and emotionally more attached to their fears than they are to their desires. Achieving what you really want to do is difficult when you refuse to let go of your fears. Being in a constant state of fear wears down the mind, shrinks your belief system, and disempowers your potential. Fear is a prison of its own kind; it's like being stuck in a place where you don't belong and you can't find your way out of.

The strategy to overcome fear is to be excited about new experiences. Why is it that people are often excited to go on holiday to places they have never been before and yet are not equally excited about new experiences in their lives brought by taking a different step and direction in life? When you take a new direction in your life as if you were going to a new holiday destination, your attitude towards your unknown life would be positive and different and your actions would be empowered.

The greatest trick you ever pulled on yourself was convincing yourself that your fears hold you back or protect you from danger. The reality is that you use your fears to keep you in danger, the danger of danger. Sometimes when it comes to your fears you need to ask yourself, 'Is the dog wagging the tail or is the tail wagging the dog?'

In her book, *Epiphany*, Elise Ballard tells a captivating story of Dr. Maya Angelou. At age twenty-two, Dr. Angelou, celebrated African American poet, discovered her true self-worth and overcame her fears in life through a life changing epiphany. While she did voice practice with her teacher, her teacher asked her to read a sentence from a book.: Her teacher asked her to read the line again and on the third time she felt embarrassed and thought she was putting her on the spot in front of the other students. However, Maya loudly and bravely uttered the words "*He loves me*!" At that very moment a complete shift occurred in her life. She felt a sense of overcoming something that had held her back for many years. She thought to herself, "That which made bees and mountains and water? That loves me, Maya Angelou? Well, then, there is nothing I can't do. I can do anything good." This thought, this epiphany, changed her life forever. When you begin to appreciate yourself wholly, your value and self-worth also begin to appreciate.

Your belief in your fears is what gives them life. Your strong belief in them is their mechanism of manifestation. Exchange that fear with excitement and your actions will be completely positive and fulfilling. There is nothing to be feared in this world, there is only life to be lived to its fullest. The absence of fear in the journey of life is a pathway to a destiny of abundance, an express way to a life of purpose, fulfilment and health. Transcend your fears and lead your desired life.

Fear is not in any manner whatsoever a form of self-protection from danger; it is in fact a form of self-incarceration from your true worth and potential. Most people find a sense of comfort in their fears and do not want to push themselves further to be more and achieve more in life. They find a sanctuary in their comfort zones, which are unfortunately fenced with fears. When you realise that there is nothing to fear in this world, that fear is merely a misinterpretation of subjective experience of over-excitement and that you can use this excitement to unleash your true self, then you become aware that you have been misusing and misinterpreting a valuable principle in your life.

"The truth is; most people who fail to enter into realisation of oneness with the infinite do so because they have been too busy looking for some imaginary line to cross that divides the human form from the divine. There is no line in fact."

Thomas Parker Boyd

THE GENIUS OF AKIM CAMARA

In July 2004, a genius made his debut in front of an audience of 18, 000 people alongside Andre Rieu and the Johann Strauss Orchestra at the Parkstad Limburg Stadium in the Netherlands. Akim, then only three years old, would emerge as the youngest and most gifted violinist of his age. After hearing an orchestra, the toddler told his mother that he wanted to play the violin. He later received weekly short training sessions from violin instructor Birgit Thiele at the Marzahn-Hellersdorf School of Music. His aptitude for music and his passion for the violin helped him memorise complex musical pieces and play them extraordinarily well. Able to stand in front of 18,000 people and play his toddler-sized violin, Akim inspired the audience, sending some listeners into tears of joy and cheering them with his water trick.

At the age of three, Akim had performed well professionally and in the most relaxed state a child could ever be in front of such a large audience. Most people, far older than Akim, with great talent and much more practice, suffer nervousness on stage instead of being relaxed and excited about the opportunity. Astounding talents have been displayed on talent shows across the world, yet most of these stars worry they may not be good enough. They go on stage with shocking nervousness, yet they sing and display talents that drive audiences to tears. Akim, unlike many people, had not allowed that over-consciousness of self to hinder this special day in his life, which marked the beginning of greater things to come.

The process by which people create fears is quite simple. They create mental pictures of the worst outcome or experience. They then mentally rehearse this experience, moulding, chiselling and crafting this monster in their heads until it sounds and feels real to them without realising that they are actually playing a mind trick on themselves. When they have completed a sculpture in their mind of this monster, they then create an experience of how they would see it if it were real, how they would feel if they saw it, what they would hear. Having created this fear in their mind which distorts reality, they then create an experiential environment in their head on how it would affect their neurology and later their physiology.

After completing the process of creating this illusive monster and constructing the experience of it, they rehearse the experience continually in their minds. This continuous rehearsal allows them to believe in it because the mind cannot differentiate between imagination and memory. As Napoleon Hill said, "What your mind can conceive and believe it can achieve." After rehearsing it, painting a vivid picture in their minds of this illusive monster, they then proceed to create their reaction or response to this fear.

"There is no illusion greater than fear."
Lao Tzu

Will they run? Will they be immobile? Will they fight or take flight? These are a few possible reactions and they decide which best fits their work of genius. When they have created the theatre in their minds of this monster, they look for a tangible reflection or manifestation in the external environment that can help them test and verify it.

Many people undertake this process so subtly, gradually and sometimes subconsciously that they are no longer even aware of the reality that it is in truth a mind trick they play on themselves. Once they have created their illusive monster, their work of genius, their creative imagination used negatively, they bring it to life, empowering it with their belief in it. From then on it stops being their work of genius and they become a victim of this illusive monster.

"Men are not afraid of things, but of how they view them."
Epictetus

Consider the results you could achieve by using the same process, the same creative imagination, to create, not fear but excitement by focusing only on the best possible outcome, the rewarding experience you actually want. According to psychology, people never really say what they want, they say what they don't want, assuming that they are expressing what they want, defaulting to the opposite thing. Fear is the opposite of excitement, therefore instead of being afraid to pursue your course, you become excited about pursuing it. As you create in your mind how you would feel if you were excited about doing this act or task you have always wanted to do, create this experience, this feeling, and ultimately create the excitement response you would have. Focus your creative imagination on this excitement long enough to visualise it, feel, believe, experience it and react or respond to it. This will help you focus on the positive outcome and help you react positively towards your desired outcome.

Although many people rarely question their fears, it is sometimes important to *have a conversation with your fears*. Establish w*hat* exactly it is that you fear, what useful purpose the fear serves in your life, what having it means to you and what overcoming it means to you. *When* did you start having the fear or when did you realise that you have this fear? *How* did you develop the fear or how did you come to have the fear? *Why* exactly do you have this fear in the first place and why haven't you overcome it yet? *Where* did you develop this fear and the series of events that led you to have this fear in you? *Who* are the people that either evoke it in you or instilled it, who are the people that have overcome this fear and you can learn from them how they overcame it, so you can also do the same. Asking yourself these questions, being curious about your fears, exploring new and self-empowering answers, grants you the first step in understanding your fears better and devising a strategy on how you can overcome it.

Fears are often merely imaginary walls and monsters you have created in your mind to inhibit you from freeing your true potential and becoming who you know you are meant to be. By believing in your fears, you fertilise the ground in which they grow; in your belief system. This will often contaminate your ability to recognise and optimise your potential. Many people have polluted their consciousness with thoughts that contaminate their beliefs about what they are really worth, what they are really capable of becoming.

Fear is therefore a warning sign, signalling that you are using your creative imagination negatively to create visions, feelings, behaviours and experiences that misdirect you from realising and using your resourcefulness. Fear has neither control nor power over you except the power you give it by believing in it. By overcoming these artificially self-imposed inhibiters you move into a state that allows you to explore your inner resources and gifts. Victory is neither the triumph nor the state of overcoming your fears; it is the state of living in absolute absence and ignorance of fear.

The Gospel of Relaxation by William James provides by far a considerably greater piece of advice on how to take control of your emotions such that you do not overreact in situations and be inhibited to express your talents as a result of a false belief manifesting as fear. When you accept that life has a far better plan for your existence than you do for yourself and that all you need to do is to walk boldly towards your goals and ambitions, then you will overcome your fears. When you accept that it is natural as a human to be humanly and not to live up to some imaginary idea of perfection, you will realise that you are already perfect, you cannot be anything else. The true order of this life as an individual is to express the most authentic self without holding back or being held back by anything.

DECODING FAILURE

"Failure is not a setback, it's valuable feedback. A success, if we only choose to learn from it. The road to success is illuminated with the street lights of failure."

The misinterpretation of failure has impeded many people from achieving their goals. Every failure is an invitation for self-reflection and introspection. A moment to re-evaluate your actions and change the strategy. No one is a failure, only the events which they encountered are failures. Failure is merely a way of explaining an outcome you did not want. We were all born winners in some way or another, and as we grow up, we grow ourselves into under-achievers. Winners are people who keep the fire within them burning, who keep their faith blooming. They are people who try to achieve great things in life and summon enough courage to achieving them. They are people who try the first time to achieve their goals; they fail at it, however they never give up until they get it right. A life-changing lesson is often wrapped in a failure.

FAIL can be given the acronym; **F**irst **A**ction **I**n **L**earning. Through failure we become better people; through our failures we discover our other strengths. Failure is a platform for serendipity. More often the greatest achievers in life are often the biggest failures in the world. Their failures not only chiselled their characters but also strengthened their will and prepared them for great success. It is inevitable and highly acceptable that experience is the best teacher, and the best teacher throughout history has been failure. Instead of being regretful over your failures, be thankful and grateful for them; for *failure is not a setback, it is valuable feedback; giving you invaluable information whenever you are derailed from your course so that you can redirect your efforts towards achieving your goals*. So never defend your mistakes, instead appreciate, learn and grow through them

The failures that you are enduring today are actually preparing you for the success that you will be enjoying tomorrow.

The wounds of failure help people focus more on their victories; they help one view and approach life more objectively. The seeds of today's failures will bear the fruits of a greater tomorrow. In order to learn, to grow, to be successful, we must understand that failure walks hand in hand with success and that failure is to success what the sun is to the moon. They are complementary, not supplementary.

Only when we look positively beyond our failures do we see their value, the role they play in preparing us for greatness, and we learn from them. It is important that one's desire to succeed in life in whatever endeavours one participates in is a hundredfold more than the fear of failing. Failure must be your wise teacher, a groomer, a sculptor and an artist that chisels away all the weakness that may hinder you from enjoying the fruit of your success. Embrace failure, for it paves a smooth road to your greatness.

Many people, if not all of us, hate. They would much rather be ruined by showers of praise than be saved by the truth they hear about themselves that they don't want to hear criticism. We are oblivious to the reality that sometimes what is bad for the ego may be good for the soul. Critics will always talk, whether you do bad or good. It is the pessimists of this world that try to find all facts about why you are wrong and why you may not achieve the goals you have set for yourself. Sometimes such situations are designed to help you reach further and deeper into yourself to draw that last ounce of strength to help you bounce back to your feet.

Over the past years, it has come to my realisation that the greatest human tragedy and trap in our lives is not so much the idea of personal achievement but *self-rejection*. Success, fame and achievement can most certainly present a great temptation; however, their luring nature usually comes from the manner in which they are part of a larger temptation to self-rejection. Most people who don't succeed ask themselves the question 'Who am I to be brilliant, gorgeous, talented and successful?' instead of asking themselves 'Actually who am I not to be all these things?'. When we have come to a greater belief in the voices that call us worthless and unsuccessful, then greatness, joy, and great personal achievements are easily perceived as attractive traits for all the wrong reasons. Self-rejection beyond other people's rejection is the greatest enemy of achieving success because it contradicts the strong inner voices. Being great is central to the inner core of our existence.

"Having a low opinion of yourself is not modesty. It's self-destruction. Holding your uniqueness in high regard is not egotism. It's a necessary precondition to happiness and success."
Bobbe Sommer

Never ever believe in anyone who tells you that your dream is impossible; the biggest mistake you can make in life is believing in what that person's statement says about you. The biggest power you can give to thought is believing it. Believe in your dream and believe in yourself regardless of your circumstances. You are the dream, you are the possibility, you are the success you aspire for, you are everything that you have ever wanted to be and you just need to take the first step to manifest that dream. When you can dream it, you can do it; if you can do it, then you can be it.

There is neither virtue in being average nor novelty in mediocrity. They will cost you more than you can ever afford in your life; success is the best option. In fact it is your obligation. It will earn you more than you could ever imagine. You need to raise your standards, cut the cost of mediocrity in your life and think of abundance and a fulfilled life; the reality is that the road to your greatness, your destiny, is illuminated on the streets of life. Your utmost determination to stop failure from stopping you from realising your dream is the only trick to being successful in your endeavours in life.

"I've missed more than 9000 shots in my career. I've lost almost 300 games. 26 times I've been trusted to take the game's winning shot and missed. I've failed over and over and over again in my life. And that is why I succeed."

Michael Jordan

Your willingness to fail, to accept that failure, learn from it and become a better person, not only brings you closer to your ultimate greatness but it is relative to your success, or more. Your failures will always be inversely proportional to your success; you just have to endure the journey. Although the world honours Michael Jordan's achievements, we hardly know the road he took to his greatness.

Many years ago, when Thomas Watson Sr was the president of international software and hardware giant, IBM a young worker at the company had made a mistake that cost the company $1 million in business losses. The young worker was called in to Watson's office to explain herself and as she walked in, she said, "Well, I guess you have called me here to fire me."

"Fire you?" Mr. Watson replied, "I just spent $1 million on your education!"

The simple lesson we can derive from this story is that the greatest mistake that people make is never learning from their mistakes and sometimes being overly conscious of not making mistakes. As a result, they deny themselves the opportunity to discover and explore even more possibilities available to succeed. Scientists have a rather positive outlook towards failure. In any lab test a failure is regarded as another data point to provide more information and insights on how to reach a desired outcome.

"To stumble upon the same stone twice is a proverbial disgrace."

Cicero's maxim

Google advises its innovation engineers to spend at least twenty percent of their work day just brainstorming new ideas. This is a fifth of a day spent only on thinking, developing their thoughts into creative patterns called ideas. Google understands that by giving its engineers an environment that does not punish failure, they liberate the creative spirit of their people. Unlike most companies, it expects about seventy percent of the ideas their engineers come up with to fail and expects that only thirty percent of them will be successful. This means Google has the highest failure rate, yet it's one of the most innovative companies. This teaches us that to endure innumerable failures eventually leads to enjoying immeasurable success.

"You miss 100% of the shots you don't take."
Wayne Gretzky

A wealthy man was visited one day by a genie that told him he had three wishes that the genie would grant. The man made all three wishes and the genie granted them. After all this, the man told the genie he wished he had more wishes to make because he had got what he wanted. The genie responded saying to him that there was absolutely nothing that stopped him from making more wishes, and if he had been wise enough he could have wished on his third wish to have three more wishes and the genie would have granted the wish. This happens every day in many people's lives; they miss out on the real opportunity because they pay less attention to the hidden opportunity.

In positive psychology, there is no failure, only undesired outcomes or feedback. It is what you do with the feedback that determines whether what you did is a failure or success. In systems thinking the most important aspect is feedback, which is taken to mean a comment about performance, usually one that is unfavourable. The means to enduring success is to be open-minded continually about your outcomes, seeking to learn from them, derive value and minimise the possibility of repeating the same mistakes.

Although the greatest challenge is to find an opportunity to take positive action when we encounter an undesired outcomes, but the onus is on us to learn from our mistakes and to make something positive out of them. In this way, the mistakes will not be a failure, they will be a learning curve. If we do not take something positive out of them, then these mistakes become failures.

Today Sara Blakely is the youngest self-made female billionaire in the world and her secret to success is failure. Yes, failure. When she was young, her father used to ask her the same question over and over again at dinner time. Her dad knew that people learn more from their mistakes than they do from their successes, so he would ask her, "What have you failed at this week?"

This was an empowering question from a father to his daughter, and Sara Blakely grew up embracing failure, not seeing it as a monster but a source of valuable feedback that she could use as a compass to guide her in the right direction. Every time she made a wrong move, she knew that fewer failures meant fewer lessons to learn from and therefore less likelihood of success in life. So she bravely took risks, trying different things. She had a vision for her life with capital to finance her entrepreneurial attempts and she knew that she had to have a good strategy. After failing her university entrance test twice and being rejected for a job at Disneyland, she landed a job selling fax machines door to door, which meant more rejection and sales failures for her.

Inspired to start something of her own, Sara came up with the idea of Spanx, panty hose that have cut out feet and a control-top. Her sales skills came in handy and her company was born. Today Spanx panty hose are now distributed in more than one hundred countries worldwide. Sara credits her success today to the failures she encountered in her life. The lessons she learned through her failures moulded her into the successful person she has become.

Sara is testimony to the notion that it's few individuals who understand that it's people who dare to fail greatly in their lives who so often come up with anything original and achieve greatly in their lives. You have not failed until you have given up on yourself and your dream. Failure is not there to hold you back, it's there to guide you to make fewer mistakes; it is our teacher and not our persecutor. It is not procrastination, it is preparation for something more worthwhile, something more meaningful and rewarding. In fact, your failures are what increase the intrinsic value of your success.

The most celebrated soccer player in the world, regarded as the best football player of all time, Brazilian star Pele, has scored more than 1281 goals in his soccer career. However, Pele did not make 1281 attempts in his soccer career to score; he has probably missed far more goals than most of his teammates of that time. It is only fair to assume that he could also hold the record for the highest attempted and missed goals in a soccer career. What is more important is that, regardless of his failures to score, he never stopped attempting. It is not the number of times you miss your goal that matters, it is the ultimate persistence to keep trying that matters the most.

Disappointment is often the result of over-exaggerating circumstances with expectations. Often people bridge the gap between reality and expectations with hope; sometimes oblivious to the truth that the gap can only be bridged by acting to meet those expectations or the goals they have set for themselves. Hope on its own without action becomes an illusion; in the same way, hope coupled with action translates into inspiration. Acting upon your convictions is the only way to unleash the greatness in you. You are not a victim of your failures; you are a victim of your attitude towards your mistakes. A student who usually comes out of the top in his maths class is usually the one who has gone through more trials, made more errors than anyone in the class. Your failures are your golden nuggets, your jewels of wisdom; learn from them and make the best and most out of them.

Recognise that you are not your mistakes and failures. You are what you make and become of them. Therefore do not beat yourself down because of the mistakes you have made in life. Instead, cheer yourself up and celebrate that you had the courage to try. Everybody says one day you going to look back at your failures and laugh at them, because finally you would have realised the valuable lessons you haven't learned from them and the better person you would have become through them. Therefore do not dwell upon them, appreciate them. They are a valuable feedback.

"*Our greatest glory is not in ever failing, but in rising up every time we fail.*"
Ralph Waldo Emerson

THE GIFT OF IMAGINATION

"Imagination is an endless journey of countless discoveries. By imagining what you could be and achieve, you move beyond the boundaries you had previously set for yourself."

Everything that is today, everything that will be tomorrow, owes its birth to imagination. Imagination is the beginning of all creation; a spring of ideas that created the world as we know it today. Through imagination all things become reality. Every object, every building, everything that surrounds us is a product of imagination; it is a tangible reflection of what merely existed as a vision, an idea, an imagination. By its simplest definition, imagination is an infinite repository of all universal knowledge and information to be tapped into and used positively by all to make this world a better place.

Through our imagination we create and shape the future; our imagination is the sunlight that illuminates the realities of tomorrow. By virtue of our imagination we have made the greatest discoveries, built the highest skyscrapers, and flown into outer space. Imagination is everything. It is the mother of intelligence, and the source of truth, the epitome of all human greatness. Through the gift of imagination we are inclined to be more and achieve more.

The circumference of our imagination determines the height of our ambitions; the height of our ambitions determines the depth of our thinking; and thinking, for many years, has been an activity in which few people engage. Thinking, by simple definition, is an art in its own right, perfected through consistent practice. Mastered by only a few, it is a weaving of thoughts into beautiful patterns of ideas. And ideas are the source of life, the source of all invention and innovation, the source of all humankind's civilisation. As Albert Einstein said, "*Do not measure a man's intelligence by his knowledge, rather by the circumference of his imagination. Imagination is infinite.*"

Imagination is the creative force and power of our souls. Through our imagination we are able to capture the evolutionary spirit of infinite intelligence and transform it into life; everything begins in imagination before it becomes a reality. The principle of auto-suggestion enables us to create the qualities and characteristics of the objects of our imagination relevant for translation into reality.

Just as the oak tree grows from the seed that lies in the acorn and the bird grows from the embryo that lies asleep in the egg, so shall the realisation of our achievements come into being. For the past century, the evidence of the power of imagination has filled everyday life, from companies that started as a spark of thought, products that sprawled as a result of an accident that triggered our imagination and turned them into the world's best products. In the modern world of rapidly changing trends and competitiveness through globalisation, imagination has become the most valuable capital to mankind and businesses. The very survival of business is now entirely dependent on any company's imaginative abilities. Intellectual capital is now considered by companies as their best competitive advantage and biggest asset. Imagination plays just as vital a role in this information as it did in the industrial age where brainpower was less needed and physical power was considered to be the number one asset.

Everything that overwhelms the human eye or serenades the human ears has been the product of imagination, from poets, musicians, sculptors, artists, inventors, writers and business leaders. All these people have relied entirely on the virtue of imagination to create what they have achieved for themselves. All these people owe their achievements to the great abilities of their imagination; everything that they have created was once a thought, an image, an idea that only came to them in their minds.

Today these people have turned those ideas into multinational corporations that employ tens of thousands of people.

Imagination is the source of all brilliant ideas, and ideas are a source of magnetic impulses. It is said that wealthy people trade ideas and mediocre people trade time. Ideas are the magnets of wealth. The more brilliant the idea is, the more wealth it attracts for its owner. Let us analyse below some of the ideas that have changed the world as we know it today. These ideas have attracted and yielded great wealth for their owners and many other people. What you believe in life will always be. You shape your life by mere virtue of your thoughts. Thoughts are a powerful force of creation.

"Your inability to see other possibilities and your lack of vocabulary are your brain's limits, not the universe."
Scott Adams

Ray Kroc, while working for Lily Tulip Cup Company selling milkshake mixers, discovered a small restaurant that ordered eight mixers. He then visited the restaurant, which, at the time, sold only hamburgers, French fries and drinks. Overwhelmed by the success of the restaurant, he went back to his motel.

"That night in my motel room I did a lot of heavy thinking about what I'd seen during the day. Visions of McDonald's restaurants dotting crossroads all over the country paraded through my brain."

It was at this time that Ray was shaping the future; in his mind he was engaging in very complex cognitive gymnastics. His thoughts were maneuvering, curling up and creating new possibilities in his mind, opening up completely new opportunities. He had a vision, a seed of imagination and he nurtured it with a strong conviction until it blossomed to what we all know as McDonald's today. Having a vision is imperative for success. Even the Bible advises on the value of it as a requisite of nature to build a successful life:

All successful people started with a vision: Howard Hughes, Sheldon Anderson, Jean Paul Getty, Thomas Edison, Aristotle Onassis, Thomas Watson. All these people have proven that imagination is the only vehicle that transcends all limitations. It is a force that makes the impossible possible; it creates something out of nothing. It is a universally divine power of nature which all forces and laws observe and obey.

The American Sports Vision therapist, Dr. Bill Harrison, has helped many baseball players become All Stars. In a newspaper article, Bill discusses the essence of having a very clear vision in what you do if you want to be successful: *"Hitting requires much more than clear eyesight (20/20 or better). It requires a wide array of skills including dynamic visual acuity, depth perception, aiming accuracy, tracking accuracy and a complex form of eye-hand-body control and coordination skills."* One of his clients, American League's most valuable player, Giambi, commented on how improving his vision helped him become successful: "Thanks to him I learned the most critical part of my hitting success…I had a great September and it was all because the ball looked like a beach ball." It goes without saying that success is a premeditated realm; build a vivid mental blueprint of the goal before working towards it. To realise it, you must first visualise it.

Visualisation is the powerful mental discipline; it is a never-ending spring of thoughts, seeds that may oneday blossom into realities if nourished constantly with faith and confidence. Thoughts are the most abundant resources available to all, better still, the most replenishable resources known to the world, and yet millions of ideas that pop into minds all over the world in one day never come to fruition.

Visualisation is a mental skill or discipline of creating a theatre of the mind and then continuously mentally rehearsing the outcome or reality you desire, putting yourself in the state of mind of that desired outcome where you can feel, touch and see your desired reality. Jack Nicklaus, the most revered golfer in the sport's history, credits his success to the discipline of mentally rehearsing his swings long before he even plays the course: "I never hit a shot, not even in practice, without having a very sharp, in-focus picture of it in my head. First I see the ball where I want it to finish, nice and white and sitting up high on the bright green grass. Then the scene quickly changes, and I see the ball going there, its path, trajectory, and shape, even its behaviour on landing. Then there is a sort of fade-out and the next scene shows me making the kind of swing that will turn the previous images into reality."

NEURO-AUTO-CONDITIONING PROCESS

This process can be done through a simple creativity process.

Start first by clearing your mind, wipe off any inner doubts, otherwise these may contaminate or distort the picture you are creating in your mind. Self-doubt can be a symptom of self-limiting or conflicting beliefs lurking in you which create inner resistances. Such beliefs act like a fog that distracts the mental path you are creating, thereby frustrating and making it difficult for you to develop a clear outcome in your mind.

By focusing wholly on the results you want to achieve, only those results you create a clear mental path for them. Rehearse continually a motion picture in your mind of how you are going to achieve them and create all the necessary cinematic effects in your mind for them. Evoke the relevant emotions in yourself of achievement, joy and a sense of confidence, then amplify them as much as you can. Allow deep breaths if needs be. Then allow that great feeling to spread all over inside your body. The objective is to rehearse it and be in the same experience you would be after you have achieved the goal. It's a simulation exercise experience.

A consistent mental and emotional rehearsal of this creative process will guide you on how to organise your skills, talents, experience, beliefs and external resources to achieving your goal. This process elicits in you a peak state, putting you in your zone. The outcome of it is a concentration and focus level that allows you to perform at your peak potential.

In their book, *Introducing NLP*, Joseph O'Connor and John Seymour illustrate how a ropewalker used visualisation and mental rehearsing to put himself in the mental state that allowed him to consistently be successful at his craft.

This process of mental rehearsing can be illustrated through an extract from the book.

"Once I was working with a person who was expressing concern about the lack of balance in his life. He was finding it difficult to decide the important issues in the present and was worried about devoting a lot of energy to some projects and little to others. Some of his enterprises seemed ill-prepared to him and the others over-prepared. This reminded me of when I was a young boy. I was learning to entertain guests by playing to them over supper. My father was a film actor and many household names used to eat and talk far into the night about all sorts of subjects at those parties. I used to enjoy these times and I got to meet many interesting people.

"One night one of my father's guests was a fine actor, renowned for his skill both in films and on the stage. He was a particular hero of mine, and I enjoyed listening to him talk.

'Late in the evening another guest asked him the secret of his extraordinary skill. 'Well,' said the actor, 'funny enough I learned a lot by asking someone the very same question in my youth. As a boy, I loved the circus — it was colourful, noisy, extravagant and exciting. I imagined I was out there in the ring under the lights, acknowledging the roar of the crowd. It felt marvellous. One of my heroes was a tightrope walker in a famous travelling circus company; he had extraordinary balance and grace on the high wire. I made friends with him one summer, I was

fascinated by his skill and the aura of danger about him. He rarely used a safety net. One afternoon in late summer, I was sad, for the circus was going to leave our town the next day. I sought out my friend and we talked into dusk. At that time, all I wanted was to be like him; I wanted to join a circus. I asked him what the secret of his skill was.

"'First,' he said, 'I see each walk as the most important one of my life, the last one I will do. I want it to be the best. I plan each walk very carefully. Many things in my life I do from habit, but this is not one of them. I am careful what I wear, what I eat, how I look. I mentally rehearse each walk as a success before I do it, what I will see, what I will hear, how I feel. This way I will get no unpleasant surprises. I also put myself in place of the audience, and imagine what they will see, hear and feel. I do all my thinking beforehand, down on the ground. When I am up on the wire I clear my mind and put all my attention out.'

"This was not exactly what I wanted to hear at the time, although strangely enough, I always remember what he said.

'You think I don't lose my balance?' he asked me.

"'I've never seen you lose your balance,' I replied.

"'You're wrong,' he said. 'I am always losing my balance. I simply control it within the bounds I set myself. I couldn't walk the rope unless I lost my balance all the time, first to one side and then to the other side. Balance is not something you have like the clowns have a false nose; it is the state of controlled movement to and fro. When I have finished my walk, I review it to see if there is anything I can learn from it. Then I forget it completely."

"'I apply the same principle in my acting,' said my hero."

Imagination is therefore a key to the creation of a reality you aspire to in your life. By imagining what we can be, we move beyond the boundaries we had previously set for ourselves. We open our minds and hearts to new possibilities which turn our fears into excitement, our doubt into will and fuels our courage and confidence to move to our desired reality. The limits of what we can achieve and possibilities we can explore exist in our words. Our words shape our world and our thinking shapes our world, our words are a powerful force of creation. Therefore the melodic music of greatness is in the magic of thinking on a massive magnitude. We must realise that often we consciously get in life what we subconsciously expected. Thus we need to operate on a positive subconscious level if we want to live a life we desire.

"As a man imagines himself to be, so shall he be,
and he is that which he imagines."
Paracelsus - Dictum

Many people see it as a lack of modesty and a sign of overconfidence to think big and aspire to great things in life. In reality, thinking big is a free commodity; it does not cost anyone a cent to think big and profoundly about desired reality. It is, however, an extremely expensive habit to think small. People who think small don't only limit their potential to succeed in life, they also lose out on the potential things they could achieve if they just thought big.

Imagination is a most wonderful window through which to see the beauty of the world. If the circumference of your imagination were relative to the size of the universe, you would realise that the sky is not the limit any more; in fact it has never been the limit. How great it is to be able to navigate the world with your imagination, taking a telescoping view of it, viewing it as an intriguing planet far away that looks like a star. Then taking an eagle's view of it, and finally taking a microscopic view of it, seeing the bigger picture and then breaking it into incalculable and miniscule pieces.

Imagination is an endless journey of countless discoveries. Through imagination you have the power not to see things for what they are but to see them for what you want them to be and then make them what you want them to be. With imagination you can do what you want to do and be what you want to be. It is only reasonable then to envision the beauty of our future and use our imagination as the chisel and hammer to carve the greatness in us until we set it free and unleash our optimum potential. We must then see the value of fear in our lives.

Our courage to move forward in life and bring our dreams to reality must be fuelled by our fear of staying behind, crippled by mediocrity. In this way we use fear as a positive force in our lives. We convert the fear of moving out of our comfort zone into an excitement that catapults us into our element, our true greatness. Failure is not designed to stop you from moving forward, it is designed to equip you with insight to overcome all odds and raise you as victor.

By broadening the horizons of your imagination, you broaden the horizons of your view of life and your outreach in life. Ever wonder why successful people embrace views, be they beach horizons, the view from the balcony of a penthouse, that top floor corner office or the office of the CEO? Those views give a glimpse of a bigger and more beautiful picture of life. The word 'limit' is relative to imagination; visionaries shape the world through their imagination, seeing the beauty of a future other people can't see, and striving for its reality.

Having a mental picture of yourself and who you want to be is the most important step in becoming the person you desire to be. Your mental picture of what you desire is a compass that guides your decisions in life and the actions you ultimately take. You are the greatness you believe yourself to be. You can outgrow the limits of the image you impose upon yourself and you can also overcome the limits of the person you are at the moment. The ability to use your self-image allows you to harness it in a manner that makes it very clear who you want to be and gives you a clear direction of the steps you need to take to become that person and achieve your goals.

It is only when you decide to stretch the boundaries of your imagination to their utmost ability, as far as the rising of the sun to the setting of it, that you will begin to discover the greatness in you.

When you envision your destiny in life, you liberate the spirit of your imagination. When the spirit is liberated, it vibrates with a higher frequency in such a way that it breaks all artificial barriers. Your potential unleashes, you discover something more powerful, more meaningful inside you that is worth realising. Your words become a powerful force of energy; they become potent with a power that crushes all walls, transcends all boundaries and reveals a new world.

Putting yourself in a mental state that allows you to see, feel, touch and experience living your dream for a moment is a great exercise. In order to bring yourself closer to your desired aspirations, mentally rehearse the experience by closing your eyes and visualising the experience until it captivates all your senses. The moment you can relate to it on that level and be part of it, then you can direct your actions to bring that vision into reality. Use your conscious motives to influence your unconscious inner powers to direct you on the path you want. What you impress upon your mind continuously will ultimately be expressed in reality in the long run. It is therefore important to consciously impress only positive thoughts and aspirations on your mind.

This means applying the fundamental principle of self-suggestion. Your mind accepts whatever is continuously impressed upon it; the strongest ideas you hold on to, it equally holds on to them, whether bad or good. Hold on to positive ideas as they rub out negative ideas in the mind, just as darkness vanishes under sunlight. Instead of repeating words and phrases like "I will not be afraid", "I will not fail", "I will not lose" and "I will not give up", remember your mind holds on to the strongest notions you impress upon it and replace such phrases with "I will be successful", "I will make it", "I will live my dream", "I will be happy and I will succeed".

Notice that in the first group of sentences, the strongest idea is 'not', which creates subconscious limitations in your mind; in the second group of sentences the strong repetitive idea is 'will', which expresses the drive, willingness and eradication of any subconscious limiting beliefs. In the former you consciously want positive results but unconsciously suggest negative results. When you want a specific outcome in your life, do not affirm it by denying a negative outcome; instead seek a positive outcome by affirming a positive outcome.

"Hold a picture of yourself long and steadily enough in your mind's eye and you will be drawn toward... picture yourself vividly as winning and that alone will contribute immeasurably to success. Great living starts with a picture, held in your imagination, of what you would like to do, or be."

Dr. Harry Emerson Fosdick

The discipline of mentally rehearsing one's desired outcome is a technique that has been used by many successful people in their respective fields, including athletes, sportsmen, and entrepreneurs who use visualisation to achieve outstanding results. According to research, holding a definite picture of your desired outcome in your mind over a lengthy period of time creates an imprint of it in your unconscious intelligence. This blueprint of the desired outcome is then tattooed somewhere in a small part of your brain stem called the reticular activating system (RAS). The purpose of this part of your brain, as the name implies, is to regulate the states of high attention or concentration. It is also the part of your brain responsible for dreaming. Functioning like an engineer, after it receives the blueprint of the desired outcome it then directs your inner human instinct and physiology, helping you to filter out all distractions around you and focus on the desired outcome until you achieve it.

The image you hold in your mind of your future, your desired outcome, is like a project plan that you give to your unconscious mind to work on and direct you towards. The mind works like an architect who builds the blueprint and then the reticular activating system works like the engineer, bringing the plan and building it. Any thought that is impressed upon the mind over a long period of time activates the RAS and this engineer then quickly works to help direct your focus to making it become a reality. It is therefore important to be aware of the mental images you hold in your mind of your future and desired outcomes; the more positive and empowering they are to you, the better the position they put you in to attain rewarding goals.

When you impress upon your mind long enough the desired reality you would like to express in your life, your instincts guide you carefully and cautiously to the achievement of that goal. As early as age six Tiger Woods spoke positive affirmations to himself that he would be a great golfer. He credits his ongoing record-breaking performances to visualisation, having a clear mental image of the course he was playing, his swings and the victory he desired. He is known to be the most mentally focused golf player with a '*horrifying precision*' of golf swings. This is clearly because of the vividness of the mental image he has of the game in his mind even before he steps on to the golf course; his body is merely the mechanism to execute the mental plan.

As your imagination expands, your world shrinks. Those who can see the invisible will accomplish the possible. Your vision in life or for your future should be the alarm clock that wakes you up in the morning, a lullaby that takes you to sleep in the evening. Your sweet dream at night and your reality by day. Everything you do in this very moment should be a step, a means to a life you know you aspire to and rightfully deserve. The only limits you actually have in this world are the limits of your imagination. By expanding the circumference of your imagination, you expand the magnitude of your abilities.

When you meditate on a vision long enough, you see the possibility of it coming true and you experience how life would be living in its realm. By having a clear vision, a mental blueprint of your desired life, you set a steady path for your instincts to guide you in the right direction. When you broaden the horizons of your imagination, you broaden the size of your world. You create in your mind a picture that with enough will you can turn into reality. Your creative imagination is your success mechanism — learn how to optimally use it.

"The great successful people of the world have used their imagination. They think ahead and create their mental picture in all its details, filling in here, adding a little there, altering this a bit and that a bit, but steadily building - steadily building."

Robert Collier

THE VALUE OF TIME

"Make every minute of your life a memorable moment. Like a shooting star that leaves a trail of wonder behind. Make every moment of your life count, because YOU count."

There are three ways of using time, WASTE IT, SPEND IT or INVEST IT and, whether you believe it or not, the cliché 'time is money' has a far deeper meaning and value than people ever imagine. By respecting our time as we do our money, our value of time would completely change for the better.

One inspiring piece on the emphasis of the importance of time realised through a series of events encountered by different people who see the value of time from various points of view and experiences follows:

"To know the value of ONE YEAR, ask a student who failed a grade.

To know the value of ONE MONTH, ask a mother who has given birth to a premature baby.

To know the value of ONE WEEK, ask the editor of a weekly newspaper.

To know the value of ONE HOUR, ask the lovers who are waiting to meet.

To know the value of ONE MINUTE, ask a person who just missed a train.

To know the value of ONE SECOND, ask someone who just escaped an accident.

To know the value of ONE MILLISECOND, ask the person who won a silver medal at the Olympics.

Treasure every moment that you have and treasure it more because to you it is special in its own way.

Yesterday is history. Tomorrow is a mystery. Today is a gift. That is why it is called the PRESENT.

Each life in this world is not only unique, it is as fascinating as a fingerprint. The moments, the experiences and our perceptions of life are unique to the individual and can hardly be replicated in another person's life. This proves how rare and different each of us is from the other seven billion people with whom we share the world. Just as your fingerprints capture your identity, your life too defines your identity, who you are, what you are here for and everything that defines your existence.

Fingerprints are designed to leave imprints of a person's identity on a white paper. The lives we lead are also meant to leave an imprint, a legacy in the world. The question we must ask ourselves is what kind of imprint, impact and legacy do we want to leave the world with ourselves? If we take a moment to closely look at our thumbs through a microscopic lens, a wonderful clue about lives is revealed. There are incalculable dots spiraling on our fingerprints. Imagine those as moments in your lifetime. What are we willing to do with those moments and how everlasting do we want them to be? The reality is our time here on earth is just as important as the air we breathe.

When it comes to life's significance, time is by far the most important commodity after the air we breathe. Sadly many people rarely realise this until they have a limited time on their hands to do what they could have done earlier. There is a saying that reminds us we must have urgency in life: what can be done tomorrow must be done today;

what must be done today should be done now. We must cultivate the discipline of using our time wisely and effectively; every moment that passes by is our last while we are still alive — we will not have one similar to it again.

By seizing the moment, the opportunity of NOW, we set an endless chain reaction of opportunities that flood us like a warm sea. We open a completely new world of countless possibilities. Opportunities multiply with seizure. The more we take advantage of them, the more of them avail themselves. Moreover, success is entirely dependent on how we use our time, how we use our time as a tool to catapult us into our dreams, how we use our time as a defining mechanism to capture every opportunity that lands on our laps to turn our dreams into the beauty of their realities. Time is therefore a defining moment in the personal revolution and transformation of an individual. As it ticks, as it moves forward, we should be taking a step forward too in our lives.

"The best time to plant a tree was twenty years ago.
The second best time is now."
Chinese proverb

In pursuit of the giant leaps to reach our dreams, we must realise the value of time, that it is the time we have now, not the time we have lost or the time we hope to have. That matters the most. Every hour in our lives is just as important and it's the finest hour of our lives. We have today to take the first step, which sets a precedent and paves the way for how high we can jump tomorrow. We have Here and Now to reach for the stars, to unleash our infinite potential, to explore the never-ending beauty of our true gifts and talents.

The time we have now is more important as a ladder to get to where we belong. It's the now we must use to make a stand, to take action and seize the power to realise our dream, to reach our potential, to live the life we desire and deserve - NOW. They say time waits for no man, and if that is really the case then we no longer have the luxury of waiting. Exactly what are we waiting for? The right time, the right moment, the right chance? Ironically, the everything RIGHT that we are waiting for is actually now. Tomorrow holds its own challenges, its new opportunities and discoveries, and tomorrow is reserved for its own experiences.

When it comes to living a worthwhile and meaningful life, it is important to recognise the value of time, the most important thing in your life after oxygen. Most people rarely allow this thought to simmer deep enough in their consciousness and there is a very short time you have available to do what you are supposed to do. Recognising what time means in your life and realising how little of it you have relative to how much you can do and achieve will definitely help you take action to achieve your dreams as soon as possible.

THE LAST LECTURE: ACHIEVING YOUR CHILDHOOD DREAMS

In his inspiring talk, '*The Last Lecture*', which inspired more than 17 million people worldwide and was later turned into a New York Times bestselling book, author Randy Pausch gives an account of his life and achieving his childhood dreams. Talking at length and in great depth on using time wisely to achieve your dreams while you still have the energy, space and time, he delivered is by far one of the most inspiring life stories on achieving one's dreams.

Randy was a professor of computer science and led many innovative projects such as Alice, an educational programme, and ran other projects at Disney and Electronic Arts. Eventually he founded and lectured at Entertainment Technology Centre, as well as a course in Virtual Reality at Carnegie. In his lecture he recounts playing on a football team as a nine-year-old boy. He said his greatest lesson in life was after a football practice at which his coach had given him a hard time during training.

His teammate told him that he saw how the coach was hammering him that day and he should appreciate it because: "*When you are screwing up and nobody is saying anything to you any more that means they gave up. When you see yourself doing something badly and nobody is bothering to tell you any more, then that's a bad place to be in. Your critics are the ones who are telling you they still care.*"

Randy did not play to reach the National Football League; however the greatest thing he learned as a young player was that experience is what you do get when you don't get what you wanted. Amongst his childhood dreams was that he wanted to be a Disney Imagineer, and to author an article in the World Book Encyclopedia, which he achieved. Randy achieved all the dreams he had set for himself while he was child and, most importantly, his greatest life achievement was enabling others to achieve their own dreams.

Randy's greatest life lessons to his students and audiences were:

1. Have fun in everything you do.

2. Never lose your childlike wonder.

3. Never give up on your childhood dreams. Even if it may seem difficult, remember the brick walls are not there to stop you, they are there to stop those who are not dedicated enough.

4. Show gratitude, never complain. Work harder and be good at something as it makes you valuable.

5. Find the best in everyone and always look for the best in everyone, for people have a good side in them. Just be patient.

6. And, most importantly, always be prepared, for luck is truly where preparation meets opportunity.

On informing the University's president that he was doing a talk about 'Achieving Your Childhood Dreams', the president replied, "Please tell them about having fun, because that is what I remember you for." Randy replied, *"I can do that, but it's kind of like a fish talking about the importance of water. I mean I don't know how to not have fun. I'm dying and I'm having fun. And I'm going to keep having fun every day I have left. Because there's no other way to play it."*

In closing his lecture, Randy Pausch gave advice to his audience and students, referring to his talk:

> *"It is not about how to achieve your dreams. It is about how to lead your life. If you lead your life the right way, the karma will take care of itself. The dreams will come to you."*

In 2008 Randy Pausch passed on at the age of 47 after being diagnosed with pancreatic cancer. His wife and three kids survive him. His life is a testimony and a lesson to each one of us that we can all achieve the dreams we have set for ourselves in life. Regardless of what happens, in the end it is not how life ends, it is how you have lived your life that matters the most. In honour of his contributions and leadership, Electronic Arts has endowed a scholarship fund in his name. It has become an endowed scholarship fund to contribute to education, computer science and digital entertainment, and to educate and empower women in technology. This scholarship has been awarded annually to female undergraduates at Carnegie Mellon University who demonstrate excellence in computer science and a passion in the pursuit of a career in video games. In addition, in honour of his contributions to bridging the gap between the arts and computer science, Carnegie Mellon University has built a footbridge named the Randy Pausch Memorial Footbridge between Purnell Centre for the Arts, which is the School of Drama, and the Gates Centre for Computer Science. This bridge holds an important symbolic meaning for the school and signifies Randy's contributions at large to the school and these two disciplines, which were seen as separate for many years.

We are not as not old as our age tells us, we are as young as our hearts tell us. So let us stay young at heart because we can be just as young and vibrant as we wish to be. In the words of Benjamin Franklin: "We do not stop playing because we grow old, we grow old because we stop playing." The greatest lesson about making the best of one's time is to have discovered in life to be happy at all times. Always find an opportunity to laugh whenever you can. Sometimes start first by laughing at yourself for taking life too seriously. And remember that the greatest gift to give to a child is to teach them how to dream, to hold on to that dream, to have faith in it and dedicate their life to making it a reality. The greatest gift to give to an adult on the other hand is to remind them how to be a child again.

"Every child is an artist. The problem is how to remain an artist once we grow up."

Pablo Picasso

To avoid disappointment, please book an appointment. And please never be late
For your appointment, it can change your fate.

The message above was a note posted on the door of one of my lecturers back at University. It is quite clear and simple, yet sends out a powerful message about the importance of time. You don't want to only always be on time, ensure you are always there before time. Most students who find themselves repeating modules do so not because of their inability to pass, it is because they lack respect for time. Many people complain so much about not having time to do that or do this that they don't have time to finish that project.

In reality, there is more than enough time in a day to do what is necessary; what people lack is discipline and knowing how to use their time effectively. Every morning you have two choices, to either continue your sleep with dreams or to wake up and chase your dreams. Use your time wisely, be accountable and responsible for every minute you invest in it. Realise that in the journey you are in, the pursuit of your dream, you are the captain of your ship, the master of your universe. Recognise that only you can write your own success story. No one else is reserved to do that honourable job for you.

When you change what you focus your mind on, then the meaning for your time will change. When you focus on negative thoughts followed by negative actions, then time becomes a punishment to you. It moves as slowly as possible. Similarly, when you focus your thoughts, energies and efforts to something you love doing, or thoughts that make you feel great about yourself, then time moves with the speed of light because you have been skyrocketed into your element where your talents and passion become one. There are many people who by 8 o'clock Monday morning are already looking forward to 5 o'clock Friday evening. This attitude makes them unproductive and negative about their lives. The whole week feels like a slow drag. When you positively focus your thoughts and energies, time becomes irrelevant and joy, fulfillment and success come abundantly to you.

When you envision your life as wonderful as the Trevi fountain, ever flowing with miracles and wonders, a true fountain of wealth as beautiful as the magic fountain of Montjuic or the Bellagio Fountains, then you become fulfilled. Your life is a fountain of abundance, wealth, joy, health and personal fulfilment; use your time wisely to enjoy the ever-flowing spring of a wonderful life.

"There is nothing outside of yourself that can ever enable you to get better, stronger, richer, quicker or smarter. Everything is within.
Everything exists. Seek nothing outside of yourself."
Miyomoto Musashi

LIFE LESSON FROM A CHINESE BAMBOO TREE

The most fascinating story of life is that of the Chinese bamboo tree. There is great lesson of life to learn from this tree and from this mystery, which most people tend to overlook. Deep in the Chinese forests grows a tree that can change people's attitudes about their dreams and cultivate in them the patience necessary to achieving them.

With a bamboo tree you take its little seed, plant it, water it, and fertilise it for a whole year, and in the first year nothing really happens.

The second year you water it and fertilise it, remove any weeds around it, and nothing happens.

The third year you water it and fertilise it and nothing seem to happen. Any normal human being by this time will have their doubts about their efforts and of ever seeing the seed grow into a plant.

In the fourth year you continue to water and fertilise the seed with a spark of hope that this time something will come to fruition, to no avail.

At the end of the fifth year, when you are tired and torn apart with hopelessness a miracle happens; the Chinese bamboo tree sprouts and grows about ninety-six feet into the sky, sky scraping over the forest. Your dream becomes reality!

The journey to your PERSONAL SUCCESS is much akin to the growing of the Chinese bamboo tree. It takes a while and requires patience, optimism and determination at all times. One does not plant a seed, then dig it up daily to see if it is growing or to show those around them, to prove that they are growing a tree. Your dream for the future is your own child. Take full responsibility and accountability for its growth so that one day it will be bigger than you and assume a life of its own. Good things come to those who wait. But great things happen to those who go out and get them.

"I do not think there is any other quality so essential to success of any kind as the quality of perseverance. It overcomes almost everything, even nature."
John D. Rockefeller

Most skeptics will call it an 'overnight success'. Only you will know the many years you have put in your effort to bring your dream into a blossoming reality was a long term, quiet attempt. Sleepless nights, countless failures, resilience and undying determination got you there. You may not be where you want to be today, you may not have all the things you desire today, you may not have reached the heights of your true greatness, but as long as you hold on, as long as you nurture the seed of your dream with your belief in it, then five years will feel like a real overnight.

Ray Kroc, although his success story was an out of the blue, straight into the blue sky kind of story, the founder of McDonald's took roughly thirty years to turn his company into a global brand. As he once said:

"I was an overnight success all right, but thirty years is a long, long night."

Perhaps you may not be living your dream right now, you may be working towards it, or you may have given up on your dream and settled for what you have on the table right now. And how long are you intending on settling for less than your real worth? How long are you willing to take whatever is thrown at you and go day by day like that? When you take a moment to envision your life thirty years from now where would you like to be? What would you like to have? What things do you want to look back to that you have done? What do you want to have achieved by then? By having a vivid picture of how, what, when and where you would like to be a decade from now, then ask yourself a simple question: 'What am I doing now that will get me there, or is what I am doing now going to get me there?'

Two strangers used to meet in a train on their way home after work. One day the two strangers sat down on the same seat in the train and started a conversation about commonplace things of the day, the weather, the economy and how their day went by. Tim worked for a company that made and sold guns and John worked as a salesman and motivational speaker. As they progressed in their conversation, Tim felt inspired by the direction that John was taking in his life, to motivate people and inspire them to be successful and driven in their lives. He told John, "You know, John, I am really inspired by what you do and how you use your time to make this difference so that you always look forward to the start of your day and in the evening you are always excited to go back home because you know you have been doing what you love." He sighed deeply and looked at John as if to release something that had been weighing heavily on his chest.

John looked at this stranger turned friend who seemed unhappy with his life and he replied, "You know, Tim, I used to work as a waiter at some restaurant downtown, not the best experience I have ever had in my life, but it helped me decide clearly what I wanted to do with my life and what really mattered to me. I used to go back home and read self-help books, listen to audiotapes and just about attended any seminar I could. I told myself that I really wanted to use my time to do what I love doing and that's how I ended in sales and being a motivational speaker."

Tim looked back at him and began telling his story, "Thanks, John. You know I have always wanted to save people's lives, work in and be a paramedic or a member of a peace-keeping mission. Now what I do goes completely against what makes me happy. I sell guns and every time we deliver the cargo to our customers I also wonder who's life will they take. Isn't it ironic that I want to save lives and then I wake to sell guns?"

John then asked him, "So how do you feel when you wake up in the morning. Are you looking forward to the day?"

Tim looked at John as if he already knew what he was going to say. "You know, John, I don't look forward to my days or my nights, I usually stop by a pub to get two cold ones just to clear my mind and to be able to get a good sleep."

John then advised him that if he continued going this way each and every day of his life, he would be unfulfilled. Now that he had established exactly what he wanted to do with his life, he should not waste time any longer; he must apply for a job as a paramedic. A couple of months later, the two friends met in the train and Tim was happy to tell John that he had quit his job at the gun company and now worked for a paramedics company and every day he got to save lives.

The great lesson of this story is to use your time every day to do exactly what you are born to do, what you love doing. People postpone their aspirations for some time in the future as if they have an endless supply of this resource called time, oblivious to the fact that sooner or later they will run out of it. Try to be just as accountable with your time as you are with your finances. Each and every second is just as important as every cent that leaves your pocket. Many treat their time the way they do when they get to a restaurant and the menu says the drinks are 'bottomless' — you have more than enough to waste. Don't waste your precious time doing something that does not resonate with you or allow you to express.

We are all saints of some sort; our talents are the message we are here to deliver to the world. Dedicate yourself and life to being of service to the world with your talents. It is the greatest honour bestowed upon us, to serve the world with our talents; do it with pride. Make a commitment to use your talents, your gifts, every day to make a positive difference in someone else's life. You may not change the world, but to change the world, it starts with one person and that person is you.

If what you are doing right now, where you are, is what is exactly going to give you the life you aspire to, then congratulations. You are among the very few people in this world who have a sense of direction, purpose and meaning for their lives. With respect to what you are doing right now, if it is not going to help you become the person you aspire to be or achieve the things you want to do, then it is time to look around, look within you, and ask yourself, "Why am I doing what I am doing at the moment if it's not going to help me be who I want to be?" Many people who are often stressed, frustrated and depressed lack this sense of direction in what they do; they haven't yet connected what they do to their purpose.

The reality one must face is that no one is more responsible for your life than you. The people around you, the people you look up to, they are also trying to find their own place and relevance in this world. When you are part of someone else's plan right now, chances are they might not have much planned for you. Take responsibility for your life, create your own path in life and boldly follow it; there is no perfect path or right path, there is only your path and only you know it and can walk it. Step out of other people's paths, they are roads to their dreams, their destinies, not yours. To reach your dream, your destiny, then walk your own path.

You do not live once, you only die once; you live every day. Every day is therefore an opportunity to walk boldly in the direction of your dreams. The first miles will be misty and gravelly. That is not how it will forever be; there will be stones, they are not walls. Turn all those stones into your stepping-stones. There will be challenges and every challenge will hold within it an equal seed of opportunity. There will be darkness and there is always light at the end of the tunnel; there will be failures and they are not a setback, they are merely feedback; learn from them and make the best out of them.

As you focus your mind, heart, soul, energy, passion and everything you have towards turning your dream into reality, you have all you need to make it possible; you have all you need to reach for the stars, to touch the moon, to soar with eagles. You are a blessing to this world; believe in yourself, trust in your gifts, have confidence in your purpose and passion for your dream. Stop questioning yourself, stop explaining yourself to people, let go of the things that hold you back and hold on to your dream. The fact is that you are here and here now means you are ready. You were ready from the moment you opened your eyes. There can never be any better time or place to turn your dream into reality than now.

One day you will be old and grey and weary. You may no longer be able to do the great things you can do now, to explore, to reach out, to become the best you can be, to make the best out of your life. Life is a gift. Every day you wake up, you unwrap it and celebrate it; life is a miracle, make the best out of it. There can never be a better time in your life than now. Don't spend it living in the illusion of fears; don't spend it locked in dogma, living someone else's dream. Take charge of your life, take control and direct your life to the ends and means you desire. You are the captain of your ship, the star in your own universe; you are the victor of your own battles, the master of your own journey.

At the end of the day, everything is in your hands. The time and place is now, tomorrow is another day. Make every minute of your life a memorable moment. Nothing is more noble than time well spent and a life well lived. So live life to its fullest; live it as though every day is your last, because it could really be.

Hold on to your aspirations, hold on tightly to your belief that one day you too shall live in the reality of your dreams. Your belief in your dream is a pair of wings that will fly you into the reality of your dreams. Any great dream requires time to be realised — take time to work on your greatness, spend time nourishing an environment deep within and without you to create a springboard that will catapult you into the reality of your dreams. Silently, gradually and incrementally build your dream and your vision because only you know it.

"A musician must make music, an artist must paint, a poet must write, if he is to be ultimately at peace with himself."

Abraham Maslow

BE A HUMAN BEING OF VALUE

"Try not to be a human being of success only, also try harder to become a human being of value."

"When we were young, we had dreams. Big dreams. We were going to be astronauts. We were going to be rock stars. We were going to win the Nobel Prize. Our lives would be full of wonder and adventure. We would save the world, we would be presidents, we would be doctors, we would be scientists and artists, we would pull rabbits from hats, we would cure bad diseases, we would marry royalty. Every night of the week we would don formal attire and go to yet another ceremony at which we would win prizes and in our acceptance speeches make gracious yet pointed remarks about our childhood Nemeses, who would seethe quietly with envy..." Excerpt from an article in Fortune magazine of 6 October 2006.

Today most people just say, well, so much for that. In fact many people have grown up to settle for far less than they had set out for in life. Are you really living your purpose in life, are you pursuing the reality of your dreams or have you given up on them? Giving up requires a certain kind of self-corruption and low self-discipline. Setting goals for yourself and never having the heart to achieve them requires a certain level of self-destructive selfishness. Giving up on your dreams, giving up on the pursuit of realising your dreams means you have, in fact, given up on yourself. Your ticket to success is finding your passion and purpose in life. How will you know when you have found it? When have found something that you love doing, that ignites your creative potential, something that you cannot imagine life without, that you cannot think of replacing with anything else, strive every day to become great at it. That is a signal that you have found your purpose. If success and happiness is what you seek in life, then your purpose in life is what you must find first.

Purpose is a designated direction of your life. Only when you have found your true purpose does being alive have meaning. Every day feels like a gift and every moment is a memorable experience of life. Better live your life trying to find your true purpose than spend the rest of your life regretting why you never sought after your purpose. The beauty of life is that what you seek also seeks you, it's just a question of how much. For every step you take towards your dream, every extra mile you walk towards the realisation of your purpose, your dream and your purpose are equally stepping towards you, walking an extra mile towards you.

Cultivate in your mindset optimum FOCUS (Follow One's Course Until Successful). Achieving your potential is a continual process of developing and training the mind to aim, concentrate and work towards achieving that goal. Set yourself goals and milestones that will eventually and gradually lead you to realising your life's vision, dream and purpose. Every day is a building block, a step closer to achieving your purpose.

Every challenge you come across maintains within itself an equal if not greater seed of opportunity. Your current challenges do not determine your downfall or success, it is your ***ATTITUDE*** towards those challenges that determines how successful you will be. Your attitude determines your altitude. Success is a state of mind and therefore it can be cultivated. Your success is a work in progress. What you are today and what you will be tomorrow will be determined by what you do today.

We all choose our destinies in life. You decide your path in the world and become what you want to be in this world. Your dreams and purpose in life are always a step away from realisation, they are always an extra mile away for you to achieve them — are you taking a step further every day towards the realisation of your dreams? Are you walking an extra mile every day towards achieving your own purpose? Stop blaming the weather, or your circumstances, or the people around you; you are the captain of your own ship, the driver of your own life. In your life, the only opinion that really counts is the one from you. Don't allow other people's opinions about you to become your reality. In your life it's your way or the highway, and guess what the beauty of that is? You own the highway too!

Each of us is born with a purpose, a gift, to make a difference in this world, through your talent, your passion or your calling. Never double-guess yourself, question yourself nor doubt yourself. Self-doubt leads to self-questioning; self-questioning leads to self-destruction, self-reinforcing and the destruction of self-identity and self-worth in life.

We are all unique for a reason, because each of us has a unique purpose to give to the world, a unique difference to make to this world. Do not try to fit in, you were born to stand out, not to live your fears and self-doubts. Our courage to move forward in life must be fuelled by our fear of staying behind; we must doubt our current environment in order to strive to change it to a better place.

We must realise that the power to become what we want to be, who we were are destined to be and who we were born to be lies within ourselves. You have the power to become the greatness you want to be. Dedicate your life to seeking and finding your purpose and live your life as the gift that it really is. Life is not all about paying bills, it is about discovering and unleashing the powerful human spirit within you to change the world.

Most people spend their lives living their fears instead of pursuing their dreams. Are you one of them?

The time for change is now. You have the power to go out there and realise those dreams because whatever the height of imagination and dreams your mind can reach, then the depth of your courage and capabilities can manifest. Realise that the only reason you are not living your dreams right now is because of the bullshit that you keep telling yourself; you are not pursuing your dreams because you are busy living in the illusion of fear and failure.

Today, embrace your fear of failure, for every learning begins with one or more failures. Mistakes or setbacks are only experiences that help us become the stronger and better persons we were born to be. Failing to realise our own dreams may lead to helping others realise their own.

The only thing that's stopping many people from realising their dreams is their fear of failure, self-doubt, which leads to self-questioning and ultimately self-destruction. By insisting to yourself that you are destined for greatness, you reaffirm an empowering self-belief. Unleash the power in you, unleash the giant in you. Your greatness lies in your hands, in your heart. Your future is in the beauty of your dreams.

By far the most inspirational and empowering woman on the continent of Africa is a Nobel Peace Prize winner and now the first woman president in Africa. She is also known as the 'Iron Lady' and led her country to a free and fair election. She fought for justice and democracy with a non-violent struggle for the safety of women and for women's rights to full participation in peace-building work. Ellen Johnson Sirleaf's strength, integrity and exemplary leadership is what everyone can learn from in order to become people of value. Born in Liberia in 1938 in an impoverished rural region of Monrovia, granddaughter of Gola chief Jahmale and daughter of her loving mother Martha, Ellen's life started off on a road of struggle, scarce means and an unhappy marriage which ended in divorce.

In her autobiography, she recounts that when she was a few days old, an old man from the village visited the family to see the newly born child and give his best wishes to the baby. As the old man gazed at the child, he gasped like someone overwhelmed by a divine spirit, "Oh, Martha, this child shall be great. This child is going to lead." As Ellen grew up, she had a normal childhood like any other girl of her age; however, she had challenges at high school in Monrovia where she was bullied and called a tomboy.

In '*Education as it ought to be*' Emile Coue advises: "*Teach them above all that everyone must set out in life with a very definite idea that they will succeed and that under the influence of this idea they will inevitably succeed. Not indeed that they should quietly remain expecting events to happen but because, impelled by this idea, they will do what is necessary to make it come true.*"

At the age of seventeen, Ellen married and bore four sons. Her abusive marriage soon ended in divorce and she later pursued a happier, more fulfilling, and successful life. She advanced her studies at the Madison Business College, the University of Colorado and Harvard University Kennedy School of Government where she graduated with a master's degree in Public Administration. This level of education in her time marked a giant career leap and the predictions of that old man who came to her house when she was only a few days old began to unfold as fortune favoured her.

She landed a job at the Treasury Department in Liberia in the mid-sixties and worked herself up to becoming the Minister of Finance four years after joining the Treasury. Political unrest erupted in the government some time after she took up her position, forcing her to leave her country to seek greener postures elsewhere. She took up a job at Citicorp African Regional Office in Kenya, Nairobi, where she worked as the organisation's vice-president. While working in Kenya she welcomed an offer to work in Washington where she was appointed senior loan officer at the offices of the World Bank. As she grew older, it seemed the prophecies of the old man were coming to fruition, and Ellen's path in life was becoming very clear, her destiny apparent. Everything happening in her life seemed to be shaping her and preparing her for a big job and challenges that still lay ahead of her. Her strong faith, belief in her purpose and the change she could bring to her country and the women in her country was unfaltering.

Not happy with the state of her country and the way women were living in Liberia, Ellen believed she could change conditions in her country for the better, so she resigned from her lucrative job at the United Nations to go home to Liberia and serve her people. She returned home and contested the presidential election of the country. Her first attempt at the presidency was not a success as she came second in votes after the then President Charles Taylor. In fear of her life and for her family, she left the country again to reside in Cote d'Ivoire where she founded the Kormah Development and Investment Corporation, which helped finance entrepreneurial initiatives in Africa.

Not giving up on her childhood conviction of turning Liberia into a respectable country with a flourishing economy and women's rights respected, she went back to Liberia to attempt another contest for the presidency. This time she knew that she could not leave room for failure. If she did, she would have failed to save her country from the plunge it was in and the global reputation it carried. Massive genocide was happening in Liberia, children were being used in civil wars and blood diamonds were peppering the businesses of the day.

"The only people that fail in this world, the only people that fail in whatever are their endeavours in life are those people who leave room for failure in their lives."

Upon her return to Liberia, she was elected chairperson of the Governance Reform Commission where she changed all the mal-administrative practices of the government and the abuse of state funds. This tremendous improvement in the way government operated increased the confidence of the people in her. The path to the presidency now paved, her childhood dream manifesting into reality and the old man's prophecy revealing its veracity, Ellen was indeed destined for greatness, to lead, to serve and drive her country to a brighter future.

In 2006, Ellen Johnson Sirleaf was the first woman president not only in Liberia but in the whole of Africa as well. When she was inaugurated in January that year, her inauguration represented enlivened hope for the people of Liberia and new possibilities for the women of her country, that they too could reach that magnitude of greatness.

For her relentless efforts and non-violent struggle for the safety of women and for women's rights to full participation in peace-building work, President Ellen was honoured with a Nobel Peace Prize in 2011 jointly with her counterparts Leymah Gbowee and Tawakel Karman of Yemen. She is also the recipient of the Indira Gandhi Prize, the Presidential Medal of Freedom, and the Grand Croix of the Legion d 'Honneur; France's highest award, and public distinction among her other accolades. Furthermore, she has written numerous books including *Women, War, and Peace: The Independent Experts' Assessment on Impact of Armed Conflict on Women and Women's Role in Peace* and her autobiography, *This Child Shall be Great.*

When you serve from the bottom of your heart, people will embrace you from the bottom of their hearts. When you lead from the bottom of your heart, people will follow you from the bottom of their hearts. When you speak from the bottom of your heart, you will touch people's hearts. When you live from the bottom of your heart, you will know true joy and fulfillment. And as you serve greatly, you shall live greatly.

President Ellen Johnson Sirleaf's exemplary life and unconditional passion for liberty have forged a template by which women anywhere can benchmark their ambitions. She is a leader, a servant of her people, a mother, a wife and, most importantly, a beacon of hope. Not only for the women of Liberia and young ladies who aspire to be like her in Africa, but also for the women of the world at large. Her journey of life is proof of what happens when you believe in your own dream and greatness. A country has become a better place to live in for women and children because one woman stood up and fought for change.

"I slept and dreamt that life was joy. I woke and saw that life was service. I acted and behold, service was joy."

Rabindranath Tagore

Each person has the ability to make a positive difference, in our lives, communities and the world, when we begin to believe in our purpose and abilities. The truth is not inconvenient that we are all just as relevant as the difference we make to this world. When you dedicate yourself to a certain course, give everything you have to it; it needs to command all your energies, passion and mind. Only when you dedicate yourself to a noble and rewarding cause do you feel a sense of direction, a sense of purpose and of being alive. We justify our existence by our purpose in this world. We establish our relevance in this world by using that purpose for all its worth to really make a difference.

"We ourselves feel that what we are doing is just a drop in the ocean. But the ocean would be less because of that missing drop."

Mother Teresa

The purpose of anyone's life is greater than their mere desires and personal fulfillment. As George Bernard Shaw wrote, "This is the true joy of life: the being used up for a purpose recognised by yourself as a mighty one; being a force of nature instead of a feverish, selfish little clot of ailments and grievances, complaining that the world will not devote itself to making you happy."

You may think you are the lampshade, when in actual reality you are the light in this world. The only reason you may not value the difference you make to this world is because you benchmark it against other people's achievements. Only when you embrace your uniqueness and appreciate your authenticity do you really start experiencing the impact of your presence.

"When you develop that and you believe in yourself and you believe that you're a person of influence and a person of purpose, I believe you can rise up out of any situation."

Joel Osteen

When you fulfil your purpose, you experience a point in your life where your passion meets your talent; life becomes a fountain of abundance, joy, health, wealth and spiritual fulfillment. You become one with your inner self; your creative skills turn everything you do into a work of excellence. Whatever you touch becomes as good as gold. Boundless passion and inspiration becomes a driving force in your life. It is your sole responsibility in life to walk on the path that leads you to your desired destiny. Your purpose is what brings meaning to your life; commit yourself to a definite purpose and pursue it relentlessly.

EMBRACING CHANGE

As we begin to cultivate a much more appreciative outlook at life as a whole, it gradually dawns on our awareness that change is a catalyst of progress. Therefore change is not only good, change is great. All change naturally has a positive intent. It is when that positive intent meets a mindset that has a positive attitude that an opportunity is made. Change, whichever way it may be looked at, it is a vehicle that paves way for progress; all progress is entirely dependent upon change. People change careers, homes, habits and behaviours because they seek progress of some sort. Perhaps they feel the place and space they are in no longer permits growth. Therefore they make an intelligent decision to change such aspects making their lives stagnant. Often the problems we have today are the result of the solutions we had yesterday which have now made us complacent. Fear of change impedes progress in lives. It is similar to trying to get to the shores and yet not willing to learn how to swim.

"Whosoever desires constant success must change their conduct with the times."
Niccolo Machiavelli

Change in circumstances is not usually detrimental to people. It is the attitude that we have towards change that is detrimental to our own progress in life. Resisting change may mean going against progress. Those who resist embracing change fail to see and seize the opportunities that change brings with it. They hold on to ideals of conventional wisdom, and conventional wisdom is often a synonym for stagnancy, a symptom for complacency, and they find themselves regressing in life. Mankind has progressed through evolution. Nature replenishes itself through seasons. Civilisation of nations has been a result of revolutions due to change in ways of thinking, in attitudes and aspirations for growth. All forms of progress in life have been a result of a series of events that evolved over time to yield the present day circumstance. Change is therefore imperative for growth and to pave the way to explore new possibilities and to discover new opportunities.

As you embrace change in your life, you begin to enjoy more progress. Change transforms life to a better place where you can discover the potential and abilities you always had but had not yet explored. It gives you the opportunity to reflect and learn from your past experiences, to use those experiences as a resource to advance your aspirations and ambitions. As you open your mind to change, you expand your world and increase the possibilities of growth in your life. Over thousands of years, nature has taught us that it is only the species that have endured change that eventually enjoyed the opportunities that came along with it. Therefore instead of being intimidated by the end of the old, be inspired by the beginning of the new. In the words of Johann Wolfgang von Goethe, "*Life belongs to the living and he who lives must be prepared for changes.*" By its simplest definition, change is the oil that greases the wheels of progress in life.

"Progress is impossible without change, and those who cannot change their minds cannot change anything."
George Bernard Shaw

THE FINAL WORD

As I write the last words in this book, I would like to wish and hope that you have derived value from it and it has transformed you in some way or another for the better. I hope as you read the last pages of this book you have found, as I promised in the first pages, that I shared with you the true principles that will guide you in reaching your optimum potential and that these principles will live in you and with you as you discover your potential.

Many people resort to various sources or references on how to achieve their goals, realise their dreams and live the life they aspired to. Of course books, success experts and the likes promise us a quick fix; do this, do that, and follow these steps and BAM! you will be sailing in the reality of your dreams.

There is no secret source to success. By weaving the principles in this book into the fabric of your life as habits, you will achieve your goals. It is imperative that you practise these principles with the right state of the mind and the right understanding of where and how to use them in order to yield positive results in your life.

Realising your own dreams and living the life which you desire; being able to provide your family with all the resources and freedom to bring joy and happiness into their lives resides in a place which lies dormant in you. That place is a place of abundance, of joy, of happiness and countless possibilities that, when tapped into, open a door to which you shall never return. It is this path that everyone desires to take. Unfortunately many people take the opposite direction. Why do you board a bus to the city when you actually want to get to the countryside? Many think there is a path to their destiny without realising that there is no path, the path can only be created the moment you decide to stand up and walk to your destiny

Over many decades noble teachers of personal success and growth have all preached one message. Although it has been said differently, their words encapsulated one message of self-empowerment, of personal mastery and self-awareness. A message so obvious and yet so overlooked that people look for complicated and scientific processes to success, when it is such a simple and achievable commodity available to all individuals.

The discovery of your greatness is that the achievement of all your desires and ambitions lies within you. In order to realise your dream, you must be aware that the power to realise your own dreams, to become who you have always wanted to be, to achieve all your desired goals, that power lies within you. Not your friend, not your company, not your family, not anything or anyone in this world, but right within you. You are the seer of your own destiny, you hold the compass of your own journey.

All venerable people who have been successful in their respective fields evangelised one principle; that your reality is a figment of your own imagination. Thoughts become reality. As you think, you create. It is therefore important to be conscious of what you think about because it shapes your reality.

This is the greatest truth there ever will be and the founding principle of success in any field or expertise; the ability to apply your mind to achieving your goals and working tenaciously to achieve them. When you change the way you look at the things around you, then the things around you will begin to change. In Isadora Duncan's motto, "*Sans limites*", simply meaning there are no limits.

The worst thing that can ever happen in this world is the waste of human potential. When you change your attitude towards your current circumstances in life and recognise them as potential opportunities, you have crossed the bridge into the achievement of your goals. They say, 'Go home or go **B**e **I**nfinitely **G**reat (BIG).' Your attitude towards your circumstances will determine the magnitude of your success and ultimately your altitude in life. Our current reality is a collective mirror-reflection of our thoughts; recognise that the power to turn stumbling stones in your life into stepping-stones to achieve your goals lies in your state of the mind.

RISE AND SHINE; Today is your day!

Maybe today you are well in your twenties
Or alive and healthy in your good thirties;
Life is a song and you dance to its melodies
And every experience is a kaleidoscope of butterflies.

Maybe you feel like you are climbing a mountain
And you want your life to be like a fountain.
Your life is like a wonderful journey on a train
With beautiful scenery; like a summer in Spain

One day you are going to be grey and old
And you will be like a book of stories untold.
You will remember the stars in your eyes,
The dream in your heart, the song in your ears.

Life would have seemed to have gone by like a shooting star;
The journey would have been that on gravel and tar.
You will reflect on the innumerable missed opportunities
And all those endless and countless possibilities.

But wake up today, take a sigh, it is your day;
You have a song in your heart, a message to say
And do it with suavity and utmost verve.

"WE CAN ONLY GROW BY GROWING OTHERS..."

Having read and been inspired by *THE GREATNESS IN YOU* you too can now begin your journey of growing others by helping them discover THE GREATNESS IN THEM by sharing with them the principles enshrined in this book. '*It doesn't take one person to change the world, but it starts with one person, and today that person is you*'. Take your first step of making the world a better place by taking the following actions immediately to make this positive difference:

- Recommend or gift, *THE GREATNESS IN YOU* to your family, relatives, friends, neighbours, colleagues, co-workers, club members, network groups, schools, orphanages, hospitals, rehabilitation centres, old age homes, prisons, societies and your community. They too will be inspired by these principles that will guide them on discovering, The Greatness in them.

- Take your time to share quotes, your thoughts, suggestions, epiphanies, perspectives and ideas on this book on Facebook, YouTube, Twitter, LinkedIn, Instagram and other social media platforms. You can also share your own insights about discovering *THE GREATNESS IN YOU* on your blog or write a book review.

- If you are in a leadership role as a chairperson, CEO, entrepreneur, business owner and/or manager, supervisor or team leader, in any role you are in you too can make this world a better place by empowering others through investing in a copy of this book as a *token of inspiration* to help them discover and reach their optimum potential.

- Your are welcome to reach out to your local radio stations, any online media, local newspapers and magazines, speaking agencies, organisations and event planners to have the author be interviewed or speak and share how through the principles enshrined in this book everyone can be guided on how to discover their talents, reach their full potential and discover THE GREATNESS IN THEM.

Take a first step today to growing others. Start your own
"THE GREATNESS IN YOU"
Movement today by inspiring and contributing towards helping others discover their purpose and reach their full potential.

HOW GREAT YOU ARE

(What you need to know about you!)

There is a drum of greatness that beats in your heart and your soul chants to it. There is the howl of greatness that runs a shiver down your spine and it excites you in the tranquillity of your THOUGHTS; there is a rumbling thunder of greatness that ignites you.

There is a roar of greatness you want to make to the world that will shake it in all its corners. There is this great spirit within you that makes the trees, the grass and the beasts of the world bow with honour when you raise your feet, there is this whisper in your ear, this gentle voice in your heart, an angel-like voice saying, 'You are destined for Greatness; and the moon, the stars and sun shine the path brightly as you stride through the journey of life...

One day...

'Wherever you land the grass will turn green, Whatever you touch will BE AS GOOD AS gold, Whatever you say and do will inspire the WORLD and Wherever you look, you will see victory and Success!' You know this, You feel this, You dream this and it stirs a storm of greatness within you.

ONE DAY THE WORLD WILL KNOW HOW GREAT YOU ARE

ABOUT THE AUTHOR

Seanaphoka Tsapi is an author, keynote and corporate inspirational speaker, seminar leader, facilitator and an entrepreneur. He is the founder and chairman of Tsapi and Associates Inc, a boutique people development consulting firm based in Johannesburg, South Africa, with a special focus on people development in professional and business skills and developing human potential and creative confidence in individuals and organisations to achieve their bottom-line results.

Having worked as an account executive for two of the Fortune 500 Enterprise software companies, Oracle and SAP SE, he is inspired to share his insights to inspire clients and audiences to reach their optimum potential by equipping them with simple, practical and applicable principles for achieving their goals.

Tsapi's keynote business training seminars and motivational talks are well researched and delivered with integrity, professionalism and captivating mature passion. In a simple, entertaining, educational and practical style, he inspires, motivates, encourages and empowers audiences to positively change their strategies for positive results. He is a proponent of neuro-linguistic programming and a practitioner of design thinking, helping organisational teams cultivate in their culture this methodology of building creative confidence for innovatively thinking teams.

Tsapi's ongoing professional development to become a valuable resource is his commitment to continually deliver value to his clients. These include a professional development toolkit of a BCom entrepreneurial Management degree, Bcom (Honours) degree in Strategic Management, both from the University of Johannesburg and a Higher Certificate in Management (Foundation for Professional Development).

SCAN AND DOWNLOAD THE AUTHOR's CONTACTS BELOW:

CONNECT WITH TSAPI ON:
LinkedIn, Twitter and Facebook

Visit us at
www.tsapi.co.za

To hire Tsapi as a Speaker for a live event.
For Seminars, Corporate Roadshows and Workshops

Email: bookings@tsapi.co.za
Mobile: +27 82 086 6310
Office: +27 11 040 4154

Special Sales Orders:

For information regarding book special discounts for commercial and social events, corporate gifts, learning, training and development, retail sales orders, social and community development or any bulk purchases email Special Sales at: orders@tsapi.co.za /+27110404154

For all Media, Public Relations Alliances and Enquiries email:
media@tsapi.co.za

To book the Author as a Speaker for your live event email:
bookings@tsapi.co.za

All keynote speeches are between 45-60 minutes. Tsapi is based in, and travels from Johannesburg, South Africa. Available to deliver his talks at conferences, corporate, and social events. Below are his keynote and motivational talks;

1. THE GREATNESS IN YOU
(Based on this "*Best-Selling*" book)
Theme: *Follow your heart, live with passion*

2. Go Home or Go **B**e **I**nfinitely **G**reat (BIG)
Theme: *Dare to dream, dare to do it*

3. THE WINNING TEAM
Theme: *7 Key principles to building a high performance team*

4. THE BRAND IN YOU
Theme: *Principles of Personal Branding*

5. THE ART OF VALUE- SELLING,
Theme: *Value-selling, Sales Strategy and Motivation.*

SEMINARS:

THE GREATNESS IN YOU – 14 Principles to Self-Mastery

3-Hour Seminar or One-day Corporate Self-Mastery Workshop

CUSTOMISED CORPORATE WORKSHOPS:

1. Team and Design Thinking Workshop

Objective: *Create team unity, ignite team spirit, rekindle the team's creative confidence and develop strategies for achieving bottom-line business results*

NOTES

INTRODUCTION

MIYOMOTO MUSASHI: The story from his book on strategy, *The Book of Five Rings*

RAGGED DICK: The story is from Horatio Alger's book by the same title, Ragged Dick

BILLY SELEKANE: His life story is derived from an article by Monique Verdyn in Entrepreneur magazine, 10 November 2009.

1. AMBITION

RITZ CARLTON: Excerpt from the article 'Cesar Ritz – A Life of Service' posted by Teg, March 08, 2008.

2. PASSION AND DESIRE

JESSICA SANCHEZ – Youtube on American Idol, March 08, 2012

3. THINK WAY BEYOND THE BOX

JACK MA's: Story derived from an interview with Charlie Rose both on his programme and at the World Economic Forum

4. THE SKY IS THE BOUNDARY

K. K. ZITULELE KOMBI: Story is from an article published by David Mwanambuyu in Entrepreneur magazine, November 21, 2009

5. STRIKE THE IRON UNTIL IT'S HOT

JOHN DE JORIA: www.paulmitchell.com

6. EDUCATION AND INFORMATION

ANDREW CARNEGIE: The Autobiography of Andrew Carnegie (1920)

7. SELF-DISCIPLINE AND CONFIDENCE

GEORGE SOROS: Soros – excerpt from *The Unauthorised Biography* by Robert Slater

8. PURPOSE AND TALENTS

GILLIAN LYNNE: **S**tory is derived from Sir Ken Robinson and Lou Aronica's book, *The Element – How finding your passion changes everything,* Chapter 1; and her website (http://www.gillianlynne.com/biography)

9. THE VALUE OF SETTING GOALS

BILL MCDERMOTT: 'The Wisdom Of The $99 Suit, Bill McDermott's story', as told by Drake Baer on November 5, 2013.

10. DEMYSTIFYING FEAR

AKIM CAMARA: His story is derived from his first performance with Andre Rieu and the Johann Strauss Orchestra, his debut appearance with *Dance of the Fairies* in 2005.

11. DECODING FAILURE

SARAH BLAKELY: Videos clips of her interviews from www.Inc.com and article by Stacey Perman in Business Week entitled 'How Failure Moulded Spanx's Founder', November 21, 2007

12. THE GIFT OF IMAGINATION

INTRODUCING NLP – Psychological skills for Understanding and influencing people by Joseph O'Connor & John Seymour - Story of the Ropewalker

13. THE VALUE OF TIME

RANDY PAUSCH: From a transcript of his lecture at Carnegie Mellon University and on Youtube, a video entitled: 'Randy Pausch – The Last Lecture, Achieving your Childhood Dreams.'

14. BE A HUMAN BEING OF VALUE

ELLEN JOHNSON SIRLEAF: From an interview with Forbes Magazine's Moira Forbes, November 21, 2013

NOTES

NOTES

NOTES

NOTES

NOTES

NOTES

NOTES

NOTES

NOTES

NOTES

NOTES

NOTES

NOTES

NOTES